LET'S MASTER BUSINESS ENGLISH

LET'S MASTER BUSINESS ENGLISH

Learn Key Vocabulary and Expressions
to Communicate Confidently at Work

CRYSTAL ALDEANO

PALMETTO
PUBLISHING
Charleston, SC
www.PalmettoPublishing.com

© 2024 Crystal Aldeano

All rights reserved.

No portion of this book may be reproduced, stored in a retrieval system, or transmitted in any form by any means—electronic, mechanical, photocopy, recording, or other—except for brief quotations in printed reviews, without prior permission of the author.

Paperback ISBN: 9798822966758

CONTENTS

Why You Need this Book 1
How to Practice English Outside of Work 3
Workplace Idioms and Expressions Part 1 5
Workplace Idioms and Expressions Part 2 11
Workplace Idioms and Expressions Part 3 19
Workplace Idioms and Expressions Part 4 26
Workplace Idioms and Expressions Part 5 34
Workplace Idioms and Expressions Part 6 41
Workplace Idioms and Expressions Part 7 48
Workplace Idioms and Expressions Part 8 54
Workplace Idioms and Expressions Part 9 59
Workplace Idioms and Expressions Part 10 65
Workplace Idioms and Expressions Part 11 71
Workplace Idioms and Expressions Part 12 76
Workplace Idioms and Expressions Part 13 84
Workplace Idioms and Expressions Part 14 89
Language for Interviews 94
Types of Skills 101
Interview Styles 105
Key Email Vocabulary and Expressions 117
Email Structure and Content 121
Key Phone Conversation Idioms and Phrases 127
Meeting Phrasal Verbs and Idioms 132
Key Vocabulary for Presentations 141
Negotiation Language 146
Small Talk and Networking 149
Social Media Terms 151
Entrepreneurship Vocabulary 154
Motivating Employees 162
Conclusion 165
More resources for English 169

WHY YOU NEED THIS BOOK

Any language is difficult, but English falls into a unique and challenging category. English has rules, but with these rules there are often exceptions. It uses phonetic spelling which also comes with many exceptions. When work gets mixed in, there are suddenly unique word combinations that require a lot of effort.

I wrote this book because I wanted to cut through the confusion for anyone who has to use English for work. It's challenging working in a second or third language. During my time teaching business professionals, I noticed that almost all of them didn't know what's included in this book and this is how it came into existence. There are key phrases that you can use in meetings, for interviews or even small talk.

In this book, I collected some of the key things you can use to help at the office, speak up more during meetings, ask for a raise, or do any other essential thing at the office. It's specifically designed to help you communicate better at work and feel more confident. At the end of each chapter, you'll find a short exercise to help you practice what you've learned.

I recommend you read through each chapter once, then a second time either recording yourself saying each example or writing them down in your notebook. Then you can use each final exercise to practice. Feel free to have someone read them to you while you listen and say the answer or write them out in full. Use whatever method helps you remember and how to use them. By the time you get to the end of each section, it's important to use whatever you've learned and to do this before you forget.

Think of it this way; the sooner you use the new expressions or vocabulary, the faster you can start practicing the right way to say it. You'll also stop feeling so nervous about speaking to a friend or a supervisor. Once you relax, you'll pick up even more new words and phrases on your own.

English speakers meet a lot of non-native speakers, just like you. As English is the go-to language for business, it's common for native speakers to work with someone who hasn't quite mastered the language. They too are continually learning new business terms and expressions.

In the next section, I have some good practices to help you use English every day.

HOW TO PRACTICE ENGLISH OUTSIDE OF WORK

Writing and reading exercises are great ways to excel in a new language, but new words and phrases require daily practice. You need to find ways to incorporate English into your daily life in a way that you truly enjoy.

Here are a few ideas for how you can use English for at least one hour every day.

- Change all your social media, email and chat settings to English.
- Put on your favorite series and change the audio settings to English, then turn off the subtitles. You can also do this with favorite movies to which you already know the plot. That way you can focus on how the film sounds without missing any details.
- Listen to English love songs. Love songs tend to be slower and easier to understand than other genres.
- Record an English conversation. The next time you have a meeting, try and record it, especially if there's someone you have a really hard time understanding. Then listen to it with headphones and see how much you can understand. There are also programs that will automatically use subtitles while someone is talking. This is very useful.

- Listen to audiobooks in English. You can also have the book's text out in front of you while you listen if that helps you follow along.

- Find some English practice podcasts. These are almost always free, short, and easy to understand. Check out a few and then listen to your favorite one when you wash the dishes, ride to work, or before falling asleep.

- Try out a sport or a class taught in English. For example, you could join an amateur basketball league or learn to paint from a coach or teacher who only uses English. This helps you sharpen your listening skills and build on your vocabulary for a specific setting.

- Do something you truly enjoy but in English. If you love to cook, find some instructional videos in English and see if you can follow along with the chef on screen.

- I feel confident you can think up a lot of other ways to practice your English. I hope however you practice, you find a way to make it fun and engaging.

Have fun with your English practice every chance you get and you will feel more confident and feel better every day!

WORKPLACE IDIOMS AND EXPRESSIONS PART 1

Idioms are a tricky part of English. They take a unique combination of words and give them a new meaning. They can be confusing, but with some practice you can master idioms and begin using them.

Use this section to learn common workplace idioms that can help you connect with your colleagues, communicate easily, and stay current on any big developments. Whatever you do, remember to keep trying. Even if you make a mistake, don't give up. English requires a lot of repetition so keep practicing.

If you keep studying and talk to your coworkers about any idioms you hear around the office, you can start to use them and make them a part of your everyday vocabulary.

Pull One's Weight

To do one's fair share of work. If someone is contributing the expected level of work, then they are *pulling their weight*. If someone isn't able to contribute at a level that the organization requires, then they are not *pulling their weight* or slacking off. Some people who do not *pull their weight* may be unmotivated, lazy and risk losing their jobs. It is vital to *pull your weight* within an organization.

I've been *pulling my weight* and it's really nice to complete all my tasks at the end of each work day.

A: Hey Kim, how is your new hire doing?

B: Great, I am really impressed with how she's *pulling her weight*. It's only been a month, and she's been working from home without any formal training.

To Go Above and Beyond

To give extra effort, especially in a way that exceeds expectations. Employees that *go above and beyond* are an asset to any company and see promotions and results a lot faster.

Elon Musk really *goes above and beyond*, working 80 hours a week. He claims he gets the same amount of work done in five years that average people do in ten years.

A: Hi Mark, were you able to complete the report we were working on?

B: Yeah, Lucas, I emailed it to you on Sunday. I worked all weekend on it.

A: Wow, working on the weekend, you really *went above and beyond*. Thank you.

Across the Board

When changes are made that affect everyone in an organization, department, or group, then they are *across the board*.

The pay raises will be *across the board*. Everyone will receive a pay raise due to an increase in production.

A: What do you think about the recent price increases that will be *across the board*?

B: I am not sure how well our customers are going to take the changes. They have been at the current price for two years now, but our industry has become more competitive, so it is quite easy to switch to a competitor's product.

In the Works

Being planned, worked on, or produced. If you hear *in the works*, it can refer to a task that's almost complete or one that hasn't started yet but is being planned. It could also mean that the task is already being implemented.

A major consolidation of our two companies is *in the works*, and this will help us gain a greater market share.

A: Are you still working on the budget analysis?

B: It's *in the works*.

To Bring (Something) to the Table

To provide something that will be a benefit or value. This may include skills, experience or ideas. It shows how someone is able to contribute to the current situation.

Joe was the right person to hire, he *brings a lot of experience to the table*.

A: How is the new marketing campaign going?

B: It wasn't going as expected, but Laura really *brought a lot of ideas to the table,* and we were able to make it more profitable.

On the Same Page

When two or more people are in agreement. If everyone agrees then we say that everyone is *on the same page*.

If we're all *on the same page*, then we can move on to the second item on the agenda.

A: Do you have any ideas for how to *get everyone on the same page*?

B: I do have many ideas, but word choice was one that came to me more recently. Sometimes the words we choose aren't helping us to sell the ideas. I have this on the agenda for tomorrow's meeting.

On Board

Another phrase to show agreement or support. We can get a department or an individual *on board*. This means the whole group or person agrees.

We need our boss *on board* before we move ahead.

A: Is Jim *on board* with the new plan?

B: It seemed as though he liked it, but he didn't say much. Maybe he needs a bit more time to think about it.

To Think Outside the Box

To explore ideas that are creative and innovative. It's not limited or controlled by rules or tradition and requires someone to think. *Thinking outside the box* creates inventions that we have never seen before. *Thinking outside the box* helps people solve problems and to follow a direction that no one may have thought of.

To solve this puzzle, you'll have to *think outside the box*.

A: How will we solve this problem?

B: I can't answer that question at the moment, but we will have to *think outside the box*.

To Stay On Top of (Something)

To be continuously aware of something and give it your regular attention. If you want to be organized, then you will have *to stay on top of your work*. When you are not *on top of something*, then you've lost control of the situation and can't quickly react if anything changes. Specific situations call for people to *stay on top of it* or the results may be undesirable.

This is an important issue, please *stay on top of it.*

A: Max, please *stay on top of this situation*, we really can't have it escalate.

B: I'm on it. We can't afford to have it escalate any further, so I will be managing it from here on out.

To Learn the Ropes

To learn the way things are done at a particular place or in a particular activity, task or job.

It will take a few months for new employees *to learn the ropes.*

A: Hey Jen, how is your training going?

B: It's been great. I am really trying *to learn the ropes* and the training has been amazing.

Exercise:

Use the expressions above to help you fill in the blanks.

1. The company's new employee training program is _____.

2. You really went _____ with this project and your work is greatly appreciated.

3. She just started a few weeks ago and it will take time for her to _____.

4. It's really frustrating working with someone who doesn't _____.

5. If we are not all _____ then these changes won't work.

6. We need to stay _____ our budget before we see another deficit.

7. It is important for us to really _____ to solve this crisis.

8. We need the management team _____ before we can make any changes.

9. Before we hire you, please tell me what you _____.

10. The current situation has affected all employees _____ .

Answer Key:

1) in the works 2) above and beyond 3) learn the ropes 4) pull their weight 5) on the same page 6) on top of 7) think outside the box 8) on board 9) bring to the table 10) across the board

WORKPLACE IDIOMS AND EXPRESSIONS PART 2

To Go Off the Rails

We say that someone has *gone off the rails* when there's a loss of complete control of their behavior or emotions. We use the expression *off the rails* to refer to someone who is behaving differently or unusual. In many cases, their actions are inappropriate and most often offend or damage relationships.

If a train *goes off the rails*, it means it has gone off the tracks and could crash or cause damage. For this reason, to *go off the rails* refers to negative changes in a condition.

I am trying my best *to not go off the rails* so I will go take a 20 minute walk to recollect my thoughts.

A: It's not good for anyone to ever *go off the rails*.

B: You're right and I couldn't agree more.

The Tables Have Turned

If someone used to be in a better position than you in regards to wealth, power or overall life status, but now you are in a better position than them, then we can say that *the tables have turned*. When the roles between two people or groups of people have reversed, then we say *the tables have turned*. They are now on the opposite end of where they used to be. It means that the person who once had the advantage in a situation now has the disadvantage, and vice versa.

This expression is often used to reflect hypothetical situations and commonly with the present perfect and in conditional sentences. The *tables have turned* is used for both personal and professional contexts.

When I first started my job, I worked for Rebecca but through years of hard work and many promotions,
the tables have turned, and Rebecca now works for me.

A: I had my first meeting with one of our potential clients today, but it didn't go that well. They arrived one hour late for our meeting. On top of that, they didn't even reach out to let me know that they were going to be late!

B: That's disappointing. I imagine you were patient with them, but I wonder how they would have reacted if *the tables had been turned,* and you had kept them waiting for that long.

Off the Top of My Head

When you say something *off the top of your head*, you speak without giving too much thought to the accuracy or quality of your ideas. We use this expression when we want to say something on the spot, but when we are not certain that the information is entirely correct.

The phrase *off the top of my head,* lets your listener know that you are speaking from memory and that you have not verified the accuracy of the information. You can use this expression when you are talking about new or unfamiliar topics in a spontaneous way and do not want to be held accountable for a lack of knowledge or a foggy memory. It is also useful when giving estimates.

I don't know the exact number *off the top of my head*, but I believe they're expecting to make around $500,000 this quarter.

A: Let's review our performance from our last client meeting. What did we do well and what needs improving?

B: Well, *off the top of my head*, I'd say that we did a great job understanding the client's needs. They seemed engaged right from the get-go and appreciated our efforts in understanding.

To Beat Around the Bush

If someone *beats around the bush*, they do not talk about a subject in a way that is open or direct. Instead, they talk about irrelevant or unimportant details to avoid getting to the main point. They avoid discussing what really matters. People usually *beat around the bush* to avoid a subject that is sensitive, controversial or uncomfortable for them to discuss. As a result, the person may approach the topic in a vague or roundabout manner to protect themselves.

Beating around the bush can be used as a tactic to stall for time or avoid answering a difficult question; this method is often seen in politics or negotiations. The phrase can also be used to tell someone to speak more effectively.

What's the problem? Please stop *beating around the bush* and just tell me exactly what happened so that I can help you.

A: He was really *beating around the bush* but maybe he was trying to tell me that he was going to leave the company. What do you think?

B: I think that assumption may be accurate but until he gives us his resignation, we won't be sure.

To Get to the Point

To reach the main or most important idea of something that is said or written. If someone beats around the bush, they will never *get to the point*. In situations where someone beats around the bush we can say, please *get to the point*. When we *get to the point*, we communicate more effectively, and people will understand us better.

I enjoy listening to people who are direct and *get to the point quickly*.

A: Many cultures speak so differently, some really *get to the point* quickly, while others beat around the bush. It's important to adapt your approach in communication depending on the country you're in.

B: I have this on my list of goals for something to learn this year, it's a really interesting topic.

In the Nick of Time

If you completed a task at the last acceptable moment, then you completed it *in the nick of time*. If you've arrived a minute early, then you got there *in the nick of time*.

We use this expression to communicate that a task was accomplished right before its deadline. If you complete something *in the nick of time* it means that you finished it right before it was needed.

We also use this expression with time to express that we were almost late. You arrived *in the nick of time* to the meeting. Using *in the nick of time* shows that we almost failed and were close to feeling negative consequences.

Luckily, I arrived *in the nick of time* for my exam.
If I had been late, I would have had to miss the exam.
They do not allow any latecomers.

A: How did the meeting go with our clients yesterday?

B: Well, I was pretty stressed because I thought I was going to be late as there was no parking, but I arrived *in the nick of time,* and everything went really well.

Race Against Time/To Work Against the Clock

We say that you're in a *race against time* when you have a task to complete in a short period of time. You're working as hard as possible to complete a task and can feel like you're in a *race against time*. This may cause some stress or pressure unless you work quickly to finish it by the deadline.

Race against time is used to describe situations that are stressful and often related to work, school, health, construction or preparation for an event such as a wedding.

My TOEFL exam is in a month and now it's a *race against time* to study for it.

A: Our boss scheduled an emergency meeting for tomorrow at 6am. We need to prepare the necessary documents for him.

B: Oh, wow—that's very short notice, they sure like to keep us on our toes. I'll notify the team and we'll *work against the clock* to get it done in time.

In the Bag

If you have something *in the bag*, then you are confident and sure that you will achieve it or acquire it. We usually use this expression to talk about future situations that we are sure to succeed in and appear to be in our favor. We use *in the bag* when we are confident of the outcome of something in the future. This expression is used for more informal conversations and can come off as cockiness, so be aware of that when you use it.

I have my second job interview on Friday,
but I've studied and prepared, so it's *in the bag*.

A: Good luck with your TED talk tomorrow.

B: Thank you, I am very excited and nervous to speak to such a large group of people.

A: Don't worry, you've got this *in the bag*.

To Get One's Foot in the Door

To take the first step toward gaining entry into an organization, a career, program, or many other areas. We use this expression to refer to a starting point; it's not the final destination. For this reason, it is most often used to describe work situations and the next steps someone might take. It is a place to start with the hopes of growing.

I really just need *to get my foot in the door* and then
they will see how skilled and hardworking I am.

A: How did you *get your foot in the door* without any experience?

B: My friend also works for Amazon and referred me. I guess they prefer referrals.

In/Out of the Loop

If you are aware of information about a particular matter, you are *in the loop*. We use this expression when we describe whether someone or a group of people are aware of the current situation. He is *in the loop* or he's *out of the loop*. The HR department is *in the loop*. If someone is *out of the loop*, then they are unaware of information regarding a particular matter.

I felt *out of the loop* during that meeting.

It was information that I've never seen before.

Can you bring me up to speed before our next meeting?

A: What did Joan say regarding accessing those files?

B: She wasn't *in the loop* and was denied any access. We need to complete the authorization process again. This might set us back a day but it'll be done.

Up to Speed

A person or a group can be *up to speed* if everyone is informed. This is a common expression after a person takes a sick day, misses a meeting, or has to join in on a project after it's already begun. For example, a person who joins a presentation that's already a week into preparation must be brought *up to speed*.

I have to help you all get your documents ready
before you see the board, but I'm not sure what
you need. Can you please get me *up to speed*?

A: I feel so lost after being out sick for four days! I have no idea what anyone is talking about!

B: Don't stress. I'll get you *up to speed*.

Exercise:

Use the idioms above to fill in the blanks.

1. Don't worry, you've got this presentation _____.

2. We completed that assignment _____. We just barely made the deadline.

3. Please _____ so we can move on.

4. I don't have the answer _____ but it might be somewhere around 90%.

5. We need to _____ to finish this by December 1st.

6. Wow, that wasn't good watching Ryan _____. I think he offended a lot of people.

7. I just love it that the _____ and we are now in first place again.

8. Are you _____ regarding the new procedures?

9. He really likes to _____ but I need an answer.

10. It's great that I finally _____. I always want to work in computer programming but so many companies ask for experience.

11. Please get Amed _____ on the new client. He wasn't able to come to the first meeting with them.

Answer key:

(1) in the bag (2) in the nick of time (3) get to the point (4) off the top of my head (5) work around the clock (6) go off the rails (7) the tables have turned (8) in the loop (9) beat around the bush (10) got my foot in the door (11) up to speed

WORKPLACE IDIOMS AND EXPRESSIONS PART 3

To Have the Floor

To have a turn to speak during a meeting or presentation. We use *have the floor* to introduce a speaker that is scheduled to speak at a specific point in time. *Have the floor* can also be used in asking permission to have time to speak during a meeting. As a result, it is a polite way to let the speaker know that they will speak next.

Please help me welcome our next speaker, she will *have the floor* to introduce our up-and-coming products.

A: Let's move on to our next item on the agenda. Maggie, you *have the floor*.

B: Thank you for the introduction, I am really excited to share our findings.

By the Book

Following the rules without any flexibility. We use the idiom *by the book* to state that the rules are being followed. Doing something *by the book* means we will do our best to follow how we are supposed to do the task. There are specific areas that need to be done *by the book*, for example, the law. If we break the law, there are consequences that are undesirable.

The safety protocols must be done *by the book* to keep everyone safe.

A: When you're taking your driver's exam, you must do everything *by the book* to pass.

B: I will try my best because I really want my driver's license.

To Bite the Bullet

To decide to do something difficult or unpleasant that one has been putting off or hesitating over. This may include having a difficult conversation with someone. We often use *bite the bullet* to describe addressing anything that's difficult, such as giving advice to someone, having a tough conversation, or even making a big financial purchase. Furthermore, it is used to discuss our own feelings about doing something difficult that we don't want to do.

Decisions have to be taken and as director
I have *to bite the bullet* and hire new staff.

A: What are you thinking is the best choice for our Christmas party venue?

B: I think we should *bite the bullet* and have it at the Shang-Ri La. It has the most beautiful room and the food is outstanding.

To Get Down to Business

To start doing what needs to be done. We use *get down to business* to express the need to start working now. It's an informal, polite way to tell everyone to get to work.

After this meeting is over, we really need *to get down to business*.

A: Hey Ryan, are you free to work through all the financials?

B: Definitely, let's *get down to business*.

On It

Accepting the responsibility to work on a problem, job or task. We use the idiom *on it* as a way to give a quick response agreeing to do something. It shows you will take care of the responsibility you agreed to. This expression is most often used as a shortening of *I am on it*.

I assigned that report to Elise. She's *on it*.

A: We need to get this paperwork completed by the end of today.

B: *On it*.

Think Big

To be ambitious with dreams and ideas that are bigger and better than anything at that current moment. We use *think big* in many situations to help with problem solving, changes, ideas or new business ventures. Anytime we need to generate or create something new, we will *think big*. As a result, businesses that *think big* will usually continue to grow.

To outsell your competition, we must
think big on our next advertising campaign.

A: The current situation we are seeing requires us to *think big*. Any ideas on how to navigate these waters?

B: Since we have never experienced anything like this before, we will need some time to think up some innovative ideas.

Word of Mouth

A type of marketing where existing customers tell people they know about their experience with a product or service and encourage others to buy that product or service. This type of marketing happens organically, and affiliate programs now provide a percentage of commission to customers who spread their experience with specific products.

Have we tried *word of mouth* marketing through our existing customers?

A: How did you market this event?

B: Actually, we relied on *word of mouth* and it worked really well.

To Bounce Back

To return back to a preexisting condition after a difficult situation or event happened. We use *bounce back* to describe any situation where someone has recovered from adversity. Companies can *bounce back* after experiencing a difficult event. Individuals can *bounce back* after going through a tough time. As a result, *bounce back* is used any time a company or person recovers from a challenging situation.

He's never really *bounced back* from his divorce. It's been 20 years and he has never gone on a date.

A: Sales at our downtown restaurant have gone down now that more employees are working from home. What are your thoughts?

B: I am sure when that changes, the restaurant will *bounce back*.

Back to Square One

To start back at the beginning with no progress being made. *Back to square one* is often used to refer to a frustrating situation where all the previous work is no longer needed or was done incorrectly. More often than not, it's because it failed.

When going *back to square one* is used to describe a relationship, it means the couple will try again from the beginning. In this case, it carries a different meaning, a more positive one. It means that the couple had problems and are willing to try to start over and work on the relationship again.

Let's try going *back to square one* to see if that'll help us.

A: We will need to go *back to square one*. We tried and it didn't go as expected, because of circumstances beyond our control, so let's try again.

B: I love that idea.

To Raise the Bar/Raise the Standards

To reach a new level of quality that people have not seen before. When people *raise the bar*, they are working at a new level and at a higher quality than before. When we get better, we are *raising the bar*.

The restaurant *raised the bar* for Brazilian cuisine in the capital. It serves authentic and original food from Brazil.

A: How do we *raise the bar* for our next conference? There's always room to get better and I am open for suggestions.

B: Speakers are a key asset for each conference, so if we're able to lock in someone like Darren Hardy who can really teach practical skills, we'll definitely *raise the bar*.

A: That's a great suggestion. I'll keep that in mind.

Beyond One's Control

Things that have happened that are not within someone's control or influence. We use this expression when we know that there was absolutely nothing else that we could have done to change the outcome. This expression is used for situations such as natural disasters, accidents, or illnesses. Any situation that we cannot prevent is *beyond our control*. For this reason, we can use *beyond one's control* in any situation that we can't change.

The stock falling 3% was *beyond our control*.

A: How did your conversation go?

B: I think it went really well. I did everything I could to prepare and whatever happens is *beyond my control*.

Exercise

Use the idioms above to complete each sentence.

1. You really need to _____ and ask for the raise you deserve.
2. The result of the election is _____; I voted and that's all I could do to contribute.
3. The new Nespresso coffee machine really_____ for the office's coffee quality.
4. Let me introduce Tim, who will now _____.
5. We have finished the introductions, so let's_____.
6. We need to do our income taxes _____, so we need to hire a bookkeeper.
7. Our new indoor playground was promoted by _____.
8. Kim said she was _____ but it looks as though it hasn't been completed.
9. The company needs to _____ in developing their new products.
10. It's great to see all the companies _____ after being closed for a year.
11. Our ideas didn't work, so we will need to go_____.

Answer Key

(1) bite the bullet (2) beyond my control (3) raised the bar (4) have the floor (5) get down to business (6) by the book (7) word of mouth (8) on it (9) think big (10) bounce back (11) back to square one

WORKPLACE IDIOMS AND EXPRESSIONS PART 4

Food for Thought

Something that requires some serious consideration. We use *food for thought* to talk about something that needs to be considered that wasn't initially thought about or that requires a lot of thinking. It essentially gives you something to think about. *Food for thought* can also be used when we get others to think. In this case, a research paper or study might give another perspective on a topic that hasn't been provided before, so therefore it gives the readers *food for thought*.

His study on genetics certainly provided *food for thought*.

A: That last research paper really gave me some *food for thought*. What do you think?

B: It really did. She presented some ideas that have never been addressed before.

To See Eye to Eye

Have similar views, attitudes, and opinions on specific topics. *To see eye to eye* means that two people have similar views and are in agreement. We also say this expression in the negative form. When people don't *see eye to eye*, they're disagreeing with one another. It's a very direct and simple expression to let someone know where they stand.

We *see eye to eye* on many topics and get a lot of work done.

A: Hey, how was the meeting at 4pm today?

B: It went really well. My boss and I *see eye to eye*, so there wasn't much to discuss.

To Hit the Nail on the Head

To describe exactly what is causing a situation or problem. We use this expression in conversations after there has been some discussion over specific topics. If someone describes a situation very accurately, then we say they *hit the nail on the head*. We also use *hit the nail on the head* as a question.

I think Mike *hit the nail on the head* when he described the level of innovation that would benefit our company.

A: I was discussing the three new prototypes of electric cars with Jim. He really *hit the nail on the head* by mentioning 750 miles as a good travel time.

B: Yes, that key fact he mentioned will be very insightful for us in the future.

Pretty Much

Nearly or almost. We use *pretty much* as a very casual expression as part of conversations. It is often used as an answer in reply to someone's question.

The school year is *pretty much* over.

A: Have you completed the report on this quarter's sales?

B: *Pretty much*. I just have to add some graphs.

In the Red

Spending or owing more money than is being earned. Essentially, if you've spent more than what you've made, then you are *in the red*. We use the idiom *in the red* to describe a negative balance sheet. It is never a good idea for any company or person to be *in the red* because it means they owe more than what they've made.

Apparently, the company had been *in the red* for a year before it went out of business.

A: How was our financial situation looking after meeting with the accountant?

B: We are *in the red* and need to be profitable within the next few months.

In the Black

To be in *the black* means to be profitable. A company that's *in the black* is one free from debt, able to hire the right number of people and with happy investors. We use this idiom when we discuss a company's finances.

Cheryl's new company is already *in the black* after only two years.

A: How is that new venture of yours going?

B: I'm happy to say our company is *in the black*.

To Get a Handle On (Something)

To understand and be able to deal with something. If someone *gets a handle on something*, then they are able to understand and do that task. Situations are also described using this expression. We sometimes can't *get a handle on* situations, which means we can't take control of it.

I finally *got a handle* on how this program works;
it now saves me so much time.

A: It took me a long time to *get a handle on* my personal finances but now I have an excess of money. Would you like me to teach you?

B: I'd love that, mine are pretty much under control but there is always room for improvement.

Come to Think of It

An idea or point that occurs while someone is speaking. We use the idiom *come to think of it* in the moment that the thought occurs. It is possible that it was something we may have forgotten or that just came to our minds. For this reason, it's mainly used in conversations.

Well, *come to think of it*, I did briefly speak
to him about the new plans for expansion.

A: Did you have any success in completing your assignment for school?

B: I did, but *come to think of it,* I have another one due on the same day that I haven't even started yet.

Up in the Air

When plans or situations still need to be settled and a decision hasn't been made, then they are *up in the air*. *Up in the air* describes when something is undecided, unresolved or uncertain. We use *up in the air* to communicate that we haven't decided yet or are unaware of what the outcome may be.

My travel plans are still *up in the air*. I haven't
been able to take any time off of work yet.

A: I was making plans to go overseas to teach English in Taiwan, but my plans are *up in the air*. Do you think I should still go?

B: You've just graduated so now is the best time in your life to travel and see the world.

It's a Long Shot

A venture involving great risk but promising a great reward if successful. However, the venture is unlikely to succeed. We also use this expression in sports, such as when a team isn't expected to win.

There were 6,000 applicants and I want
them to choose me but *it's a long shot*.

A: Were you able to book tickets to the world cup soccer game on Saturday?

B: No, but I knew *it was a long shot*. Seats sold out in 15 minutes.

To Put One's Best Foot Forward

To try as hard as possible to do something that's difficult. We use this expression to really emphasize that we tried our best to do everything we could have done. When we say, "I *put my best foot forward*" then we believe that there was nothing else that we could have done.

I *put my best foot forward* working towards my goal
to be an entrepreneur and run my own business.

A: I really believe that the marketing team at Coca-Cola *put their best foot forward* trying to create a new creative Christmas campaign.

B: Every year they have a new, more creative way to incorporate the holiday into their commercials and branding.

A Lot on One's Plate

When we have a lot to do and to cope with, then there is *a lot on our plate*. This might involve a high level of stress and emotion. This expression explains itself by the visual aid of thinking about a plate overflowing with food—some food might be falling off of the plate, and we can only put so much onto the plate. This is an analogy for how we can feel when there is too much to do and not enough time; that is, we have *a lot on our plate*.

I can't take that on now; I've got *a lot on my plate* already but give me an extra week and then I can help.

A: Are you free on the weekend to go see a movie?

B: I have *a lot on my plate* at the moment, so let's plan to go the following weekend.

Out of the Woods

Out of difficulties, danger or trouble. *Out of the woods* is often used to express a point of difficulty in the past that we have overcome. It can be used in any situation that marks the end of trouble or difficulty. It alludes to actually being lost in the forest.

In 2008, we experienced a recession,
but now we're *out of the woods*.

A: Have you touched base with the lawyer regarding the sale of our house?

B: Yes, the sale has been finalized and we are *out of the woods*.

Around the Clock

All day and all night. Something can be done *around the clock*, such as working, sleeping, studying and so on. Whenever something has continued for a long period of time, we use the idiom *around the clock*. There is a mental image of the hands moving around the clock continuously for an extended period of time.

I've got a team working *around the clock* to solve this problem.

A: Have you finished correcting all the midterm assignments?

B: I was able to finish, but I had to work *around the clock* to return them before the end of the semester.

Exercise:

Use your new idioms to fill in the blanks.

1. Can we talk for a bit? I really don't _____ with you on something and would like to have a quick chat.
2. You really _____ describing our new team dynamics.
3. You really gave me _____ this week after discussing those innovations.
4. We are finally _____ after working _____ for a week straight.
5. I am still _____ about who to hire for the new role.
6. _____, she'd be great to talk to about opportunities in the city.
7. I _____ didn't sleep last night because our company is _____. We need to _____.
8. I had _____ but I really _____.
9. _____ but I think it'll work.

Answer Key:

(1) see eye to eye (2) hit the nail on the head (3) food for thought (4) out of the woods, around the clock (5) up in the air (6) Come to think of it (7) pretty much, in the red, get a handle on it (8) a lot on my plate, put my best foot forward (9) It's a long shot

WORKPLACE IDIOMS AND EXPRESSIONS PART 5

Tread Water

When someone is in an unsatisfactory situation where they are not progressing and continue to do the same thing. This situation means that someone has failed to advance or make any progress. It can be very frustrating to *tread water* because we have put the time and effort in but are not seeing the results.

I could either *tread water* until I am promoted,
or I could look for another job.

A: How is your company doing?

B: We are really doing well at the moment, after *treading water* for a couple years we are starting to see some real profit.

To Hit Hard/Hit Me Hard

To affect someone's emotions strongly.
The employees were all *hit hard* by the layoffs.
The layoffs *hit me hard*.

A: Have you been over to visit Julie this past week to see how she's doing?

B: Yeah, I went there every day. She keeps asking me to come back because she was really *hit hard* by the accusations of her dishonesty.

To Have One's Work Cut Out for Them

To be faced with a difficult task. We use this expression to talk about something that's difficult at the moment and may take a great amount of time and energy to complete.

We have to move offices so I will really *have my work cut out for me*. It might be a good idea to hire a moving company.

A: When is the gymnastics competition?

B: It's only a month away, I really *have my work cut out for me*.

Burnout/To Burn Out

A state of physical or mental collapse caused by overwork and stress.. This is a term used to accurately describe a state of total exhaustion in all areas of life. Many people who are *burned out* need to take time off of work to recover.

Last year I *burned out* after working every day for three months straight. I should have taken more time off.

A: Where has Helen been last month? I haven't seen her at all.

B: She had to take some time off because she was experiencing *burnout*.

To Burn the Candle at Both Ends

To overwork or exhaust oneself, typically staying up late at night and waking up early while taking no breaks. A high level of stress and *burning the candle at both ends* may lead to burnout if it's not managed properly. However, it's great to outwork everyone and manage a high level of productivity while taking breaks. There are times in life when everyone needs to *burn the candle at both ends*, especially if you have children.

This year I have had many times where I've needed to *burn the candle at both ends*. All that work has paid off because it led me to a great position in my company.

A: Have you been studying all night?

B: Yeah, I am *burning the candle at both ends* trying to understand Calculus.

Set in Stone

Very difficult or impossible to change. We use the phrase *set in stone* when we can't change something that has already been decided or planned. We emphasize *set in stone* when we also don't want to change our plans, dates, or decisions. Some people make plans that are *set in stone* and if we try to change them, they become very upset.

The schedule isn't *set in stone*, but we'd like to stick pretty close to it.

A: I can't make dinner on Sunday night for Mom's birthday.

B: Well, that isn't good, those plans were *set in stone* a month ago. What changed?

A: I'm feeling sick and think I should stay home to avoid passing it on to anyone else.

To Throw in the Towel

To quit or give up because you are defeated or no longer want to keep trying. This phrase comes from boxing, in which a fighter indicates surrender by throwing a towel into the ring. We now use *throw in the towel* to describe when we are done fighting for what we initially wanted.

Learning a new language can be difficult, but don't *throw in the towel* just yet, you'll grasp it soon.

A: Are you sure you want *to throw in the towel* after eight months in this role?

B: Yup, I am sure.

To Step Up to the Plate

To take responsibility for something that needs to be done. This is a reference to baseball where the batter needs to stand next to home plate in order to hit the ball to score a point. The same is expressed when people need to take responsibility and do something. *Step up to the plate* is used in all situations where a change needs to happen.

Thank you for *stepping up to the plate* and helping dad arrange his house and move!

Below Par

Below average and not as good as desired, required or expected. It is never a good thing to be *below par*. Everyone should aim for excellence not to be *below par*. We use this expression to evaluate performance, quality, timeliness, execution, and many other areas where we have an already existing expectation.

This research paper you handed in on Friday is *below par*. Has something happened that has affected your performance at school? I know you can do better than this.

A: How have our sales been over the last few months?

B: They've been *below par* due to the recession.

To Fall Short

To fail to meet an expectation or standard. We use this expression to describe that we failed at something in life. We *fall short* whenever we have failed to do what was expected of us or we expected from ourselves. At times everyone *falls short*.

I *fell short* on the financial targets last month.
I need to reevaluate where we went wrong.

A: Now where did we *fall short*?

B: The customers were expecting a more consistent product and through the customer service surveys, we found that the products weren't consistent.

To Keep (Something) Under Wraps

A secret that is only known by a few people and that they shouldn't tell anyone. There are many times in life that we need to *keep something under wraps*. This information cannot be revealed until sometime in the future. If you are able *to keep something under wraps*, people will trust you.

Phil will be moving to a new department on Friday but *keep this under wraps* as it's not common knowledge.

A: Why do we need to *keep this under wraps*?

B: We are worried about grandma's health and don't want her to be stressed, so we won't tell anyone.

A: Great, my lips are sealed.

Lips are Sealed

Used to convey that one will not discuss or reveal something. In this expression, we are agreeing to not discuss a specific topic with anyone. We will essentially keep a secret.

You need to promise that *your lips are sealed*.

A: Have you told anyone about my trip to Europe?

B: Nope, no one. *My lips are sealed.*

To Have One's Voice Heard

To ensure that one's opinion, idea, or point of view is heard, understood or has an impact, especially within competing voices or opinions. This expression conveys that we've been heard and that we said exactly what we needed to. It doesn't always mean that the decisions will be in our favor; it just means we were able to communicate what we needed to so everyone understood.

If you want *to have your voice heard*,
then you will need to speak up in meetings.

A: You did great during our brainstorming session. I really believe you *got your voice heard* and they will take your suggestions into consideration.

B: Thank you. I've never spoken up at the office but working from home has really helped me feel more comfortable and engaged during meetings.

Exercise:

Use your new idioms to complete each phrase.

1. You must speak up in order to have your _____.

2. The new company policy is _____ and won't change.

3. She didn't get the job and it really _____.

4. Many college students_____when they had to shift to online learning.

5. I am _____ at my current job; it's time for me to look for a new one.

6. The budget _____ this month and we owe $10,000.

7. I will let you know what Emma told me, but you need to _____.

8. I appreciate how Rob has _____ and taken on such a huge project.

9. One of their employees experienced _____ after experiencing a lot of stress.

10. My performance last week was _____ and I couldn't sleep for a week because I thought I'd tried my best.

11. He's been _____and has achieved a lot in such a short period of time.

Answer Key:

(1) voice heard (2) set in stone (3) hit her hard (4) threw in the towel (5) treading water (6) fell short (7) keep this under wraps (8) stepped up to the plate (9) burnout (10) below par (11) burning the candle at both ends

WORKPLACE IDIOMS AND EXPRESSIONS PART 6

To Fall Through the Cracks

To be overlooked. If something *falls through the cracks*, this means that it wasn't noticed or dealt with. It is important not to let things in life *fall through the cracks*. If we are on top of what we need to do, then we won't allow anything *to fall through the cracks*. However, as a new employee without proper training, you may accidentally let something *fall through the cracks*.

I never made a spending budget and now my finances have *fallen through the cracks*.

A: How did he let his grades *fall through the cracks*?

B: Honestly, he was distracted playing video games and never noticed until it was too late. He still has time and can work on raising them.

Ahead of the Pack

To be more successful than other people who are trying to achieve the same things as you. It usually requires a lot of hard work and consistency to be *ahead of the pack*. Some people are fine with being average, but others are always *ahead of the pack*. This expression can also be used for businesses.

Coca-Cola was always *ahead of the pack* with marketing and sales.

A: Are you sure we're still *ahead of the pack*?

B: Yes, that is what the numbers are saying.

To Cut to the Chase

To discuss or deal with the most important aspects of a subject without wasting time on things that are not important. When we ask people to *cut to the chase*, it can sound rude but when we say, "I'll just cut to the chase," it means, I will discuss the most important details first.

I'll *cut to the chase* and just give you the short version.

A: I really liked how the CEO *cut to the chase* and spoke directly about the new markets we will enter. What do you think?

B: It was great!

Keep Your Eye on the Prize

When someone keeps their attention on what they are trying to achieve, even when it is difficult. They have a clear vision of what they want, so they *keep their eye on the prize*.

Keep your eye on the prize and think about how healthy you will be after running every day on the treadmill.

A: It's really hard to put in 16-hour days, five days a week, and I'm only getting paid for 8-hour days.

B: Just keep your *eye on the prize* and continue pushing through.

Make a Cold Call

Cold calling is a technique in which a salesperson contacts individuals who have not previously expressed interest in the offered products or services. *Cold calling* typically refers to solicitation by phone or telemarketing, but can also involve in-person visits, such as with door-to-door salespeople. Anytime someone is being sold something unexpectedly, it is *cold calling*.

Cold calling isn't working anymore; no one answers calls from unidentified numbers because there are too many scams.

A: How did your *cold calling* go today? I saw your sales numbers increase last week.

B: It went really well, and I got a number of sales from the prospect list.

Stay on Top of

In control of a situation and aware of changes. When someone *stays on top of things*, then they are in complete control and have the situation handled. The best leaders *stay on top of things,* so their team is well prepared and organized for every task.

Our team lead really *stayed on top of* communication when we all had to work from home.

A: How are you able to *stay on top of* everything? You work full time, have three kids, study and volunteer.

B: I am really organized and stick to a strict schedule, and it works really well.

Smooth Sailing

For something to be easy and without problems. It is really enjoyable when specific events in life are *smooth sailing*. However, there are many situations that aren't *smooth sailing*, requiring effort to solve problems that occur.

Changing the kids to a new school has been *smooth sailing*.

A: How was your time in Panama last month?

B: It was *smooth sailing*. Everything we planned went exactly how we wanted it to.

Have an Impact On

To affect or influence someone or something.

Electric cars have *had an impact on* the environment.

A: Which aspect of the conference *had the biggest impact on you*?

B: I'd say the part on Artificial Intelligence *had the biggest impact on me* because the speaker covered the exact topic I've been so confused about for the last few months.

Get off on the Right Foot

Make a good start at something, especially a task or relationship. Good first impressions help *get us off on the right foot*. This is important in many situations where we are meeting people for the first time.

I'd say I am *getting off on the right foot*.

A: How was your meeting last week?

B: We really *got off on the right foot*, I am really looking forward to working with her.

On the Money

Accurate and correct. This expression helps us to understand that someone is saying the exact right thing at the right time. It tells the person that they are correct and that you agree with what they are saying.

His explanation was *on the money*. I understood everything.

A: How did work go today?

B: I had a meeting with my team, and they provided suggestions that were right *on the money*.

Coming Down the Pipe

Coming in the future or it will happen in the near future. Something that is *coming down the pipe* will be seen in the future and worked on soon.

We can expect to see a new product launch *coming down the pipe*.

A: Can you tell me more about the quality control measures we have set recently?

B: Here are the current measures we have. There will be more *coming down the pipe* as we continue to make improvements to our products.

Connect the Dots

When a company puts various facts and ideas together in order to see the whole picture or to understand something globally. In business, when we need to *connect the dots*, we analyze the data and facts to make decisions and conclusions that are best for the business.

As we move forward, we will need to *connect the dots*.

A: Did you get the job in the accounting department?

B: Once I started to *connect the dots*, I realized I was the most qualified candidate and they offered me the position.

Exercise:

Review your idioms by filling in the blanks.

1. How did we let this _____?
2. It appears that our school is_____.
3. Let me_____and talk about what happened.
4. To be successful, we really need to _____.
5. Instead of talking to our regular customers, let's _____ instead.
6. That was quite impressive how he was able to _____ when he was so busy.
7. Owning a rental property hasn't been _____ because there has been so many problems.
8. I hope that they get along and _____.
9. His explanation was great. It was really _____.
10. We need to _____ and move forward with our plans.
11. There are so many exciting ideas _____.
12. Our presentation was insightful and really _____.

Answer key:

(1) fall through the cracks (2) ahead of the pack (3) cut to the chase (4) keep an eye on the prize (5) make cold calls (6) stay on top of things (7) smooth sailing (8) get off on the right foot (9) on the money (10) connect the dots (11) coming down the pipe (12) made an impact

WORKPLACE IDIOMS AND EXPRESSIONS PART 7

From the Ground Up

To work on something from the very beginning. When we do something *from the ground up*, it means that everything will be affected and everyone needs to be involved in the changes. As a result, each person will work towards a common goal.

All of our systems will be replaced *from the ground up*.

A: How will we focus on the new campaign?

B: We will need to work it *from the ground up*, developing completely new ideas and messages.

From Day One

From the very beginning. We use *from day one* to explain that something has always been the same since we started.

I've been interested in entrepreneurship *from day one* and want to build an amazing company one day.

A: She's been an amazing student *from day one* and asks for very little help.

B: I love to hear that! Thank you.

Up and Running

In operation or functioning. *Up and running* can refer to machinery, projects, programs, processes, or anything that has been implemented and started.

Our new training programs are *up and running*.

A: What needs to be done to get the car wash *up and running* again? Every day that it's broken is money being lost, especially at this location where we average 400 cars per day.

B: We're waiting on parts. All part manufacturers are short on inventory, so all we can do is wait. Hopefully, it will be *up and running* again soon.

On the Ball

Aware of any changes, ideas, methods, or trends and quick to react to them. We use *on the ball* when people are aware of what is happening at the current moment. They are prepared and know what is happening and what to do in the future.

I am really *on the ball* today; I slept so well last night.

A: Thank you for sharing your information with my team, you are really *on the ball*.

B: Thank you! My team did a lot of the work, so I was able to get it to you efficiently.

Get the Ball Rolling

To set an activity in motion and start doing something. We use *get the ball rolling* to explain that a person or team needs to start doing something. This can be used as advice or to simply explain the current situation.

She needs to *get the ball rolling* and apply to more universities.

A: How can we *get the ball rolling* on advertising our new product?

B: We need to start a campaign.

The Ball is in Your Court

It's your responsibility now and it's up to you. This expression makes reference to playing sports, in particular tennis. When we have the ball, we have the opportunity to score. Therefore, when *the ball is in your court*, you now have the responsibility but also the opportunity to do something great. When *the ball is in your court*, you need to do your part in producing the results that are expected of you.

The ball is in your court to decide which career path you'd like to take. There are so many amazing careers and I know you'll succeed at any of them.

A: I have to make a tough decision about which company to work for. I got offers from two very reputable companies and am finding it difficult to accept one. I know this is a great position to be in, but I just don't know what to do.

B: *The ball is in your court* at this point. Either company you choose will produce the opportunity and experience that you've been looking for.

Drop the Ball

To make a mistake and to mishandle things. If we have *dropped the ball*, then we have made a mistake in some way. It is better to stay on top of everything and not *drop the ball*. It can be very embarrassing if we drop the ball, especially in a work setting. Co-workers may have been expecting you to give answers they needed but didn't receive them because you *dropped the ball*. Customers may have needed a response, but you didn't respond, so you *dropped the ball.*

She *dropped the ball* and forgot to register her vehicle, so the police issued her a $243 ticket.

A: Wow, how did you *drop the ball* again? I can't keep covering for you. You need to step up to the plate.

B: I know, I am sorry, and I promise it won't happen again.

Caught Me Off Guard

To surprise someone, especially in a way that makes the person feel confused, uncertain, or slightly embarrassed. Someone can be *caught off guard* if they are asked a certain question or are part of a discussion where the focus is on them.

Her question really *caught me off guard,* she was very direct.

A: My surprise birthday party *caught me off guard.* I wasn't expecting anything and it was so nice that everyone did that for me.

B: Aww we're so happy you enjoyed it.

Ahead of Time

In advance and early. It is always a good idea to arrive ahead of time or to complete tasks *ahead of time.* When we do what needs to be done *ahead of time*, we have a lot less stress in our lives. If we don't complete tasks *ahead of time*, then we leave them to the last minute.

Being prepared with appropriate graphics *ahead of time* is a great idea.

A: Would it be possible to complete this work *ahead of time*?

B: That's possible, but the team will have to work around the clock to get it completed.

Red Tape

Official, bureaucratic rules or methods that are typically overly strict, convoluted, or tedious. Sometimes companies that are very political have a lot of *red tape*. Small changes within these organizations need many levels of approval. So, there's a lot of *red tape* before anything is approved.

Our lawyer was able to cut through the *red tape* and get us the answers we needed.

A: How do we get through all the *red tape*?

B: Let me speak with the head office. I know some people who can help us there.

Exercise:

Use your new expressions to fill in the blanks.

1. The new factory is _____ and has been very successful.
2. The upcoming price adjustments will be applied _____.
3. Let's _____ by setting up a website.
4. Your comments really _____ during the meeting.
5. Our team is really good at anticipating problems. We are _____.
6. There's so much _____ in a large corporation.
7. Thank you for completing this presentation _____.
8. The system needs to be built _____.
9. He has been rude to me _____.
10. I really _____ because the last month was so busy.
11. _____ so it's up to you to take the opportunity now.

Answer key:

(1) up and running (2) across the board (3) get the ball rolling (4) caught me off guard (5) on the ball (6) red tape (7) ahead of time (8) from the ground up (9) from day one (10) dropped the ball (11) The ball is in your court.

WORKPLACE IDIOMS AND EXPRESSIONS PART 8

Go the Extra Mile

To make more effort than is expected of you. We use this expression to explain a situation where someone did more than expected. It's the best to have employees or people in our lives that are willing to *go the extra mile*. It is also very important for us to *go the extra mile* for others even when it's difficult.

I really enjoy *going the extra mile* and seeing how it adds to my success.

A: Is there someone that will *go the extra mile*?

B: We have a number of employees that are consistently *going the extra mile*.

Bounce Some Ideas Off of You

Bouncing an idea off a person means requesting that the person give a somewhat immediate response or gut reaction to your idea. We use bounce *some ideas off of you* to let the other person know we are looking for their opinion or response to something we need help with. More often than not, when someone needs to bounce ideas off of us, they come to conclusions on their own. We usually have a preference for the person we choose to *bounce ideas off of*. Some people are just better to *bounce ideas off of*.

Do you have a minute for me to *bounce some ideas off of you*?

A: I'm sorry that I am always *bouncing ideas off of you*!

B: No worries, I'm just happy that I can help you get clarity.

Bring to the Table

To provide something that will be a benefit. It focuses mostly on specific skills or attributes. This expression is used within a business context when someone honestly wants to know how the service or product is better than others. What makes you different from other companies within the same industry? As an employee, it is the same type of question, but an employer would like to know what skills you have that will be needed for the job.

Cooper really was a great person to hire as *he brings* tons of experience and some really important, valuable skills *to the table.*

A: Why should we pick your company? What do you *bring to the table* that's different from the others?

B: That's a great question. We have a 25-year track record that none of our competitors have, so we bring invaluable experience. With this experience, we have a customer retention rate of over 90%.

The Bottom Line

The ultimate outcome of a situation. The bottom line is used to focus on the most important facts of a situation and can be used as a summary or before going into more detail. Usually, it is used if there is a subject that needs some kind of explanation where the listener may be confused or needs a summary.

The bottom line is when you work hard and study for your exams, you will do well this year.

A: Now you know all the information about what happened in the last few months, what do you think we need to do moving forward?

B: *The bottom line* is we didn't follow what we've always done, so there will be an adjustment period. The tradesmen need to adapt to the current measures, and this will be successful. If they refuse to adjust, then we need to find new tradesmen who are willing to do the job we need to get done.

Cross the Line

To go beyond what is proper or acceptable. Often, we *cross the line* when we offend or hurt other people with what we have done or said. In business, when companies have crossed the line, they may have said offensive comments, broken laws, or participated in unethical behaviors. There are boundaries in place to be followed, so when people or companies *cross the line*, there are consequences.

Without strict regulations, some companies may *cross the line*.

A: Do you think we *crossed the line*?

B: No, we're following the rules and got the results we were looking for.

Go Down Swinging

To continue to fight or to make a strong, determined effort even though you are likely to fail or lose. We use *go down swinging* to emphasize that we did our best until the end.

He really *went down swinging* even though it was a defeat in the end.

A: He really *went down swinging*. He gave his best effort in trying to find a job in finance.

B: Yeah, but I think he will be really good where he's at right now. He will be teaching finance, which will be great for him.

Practice:

Now use the above expressions to fill in the blanks.

1. Please make sure that George is _____ on the changes we've made.

2. Do you have a minute for me to _____?

3. I am _____ since I went on vacation, can you bring me up to speed?

4. I really appreciate that you _____ for our anniversary.

5. We can't _____. It is really important we follow the guidelines so everyone is safe.

6. I won't quit, I'll work as hard as I can and _____.

7. _____ is that we still need to work hard to see the results we want.

8. Helen _____ with all of her previous experience.

Answer key:

(1) up to speed (2) bounce some ideas off of you (3) out of the loop (4) went the extra mile (5) cross the line (6) go down swinging (7) The bottom line (8) brings lots to the table

WORKPLACE IDIOMS AND EXPRESSIONS PART 9

My Hands are Tied

When someone is unable to act freely because a rule or law prevents them from doing so. When we use, *my hands are tied*, we are explaining that we can't do anything because of circumstances beyond our control, like specific policies that won't allow it.

I'd like to raise the salaries of specific members on my team, but *my hands are tied*.

A: How will we move forward with his pay raise? *Our hands are tied.*

B: There are exceptions in cases like these where, if we are able to prove our case, then he will get the raise that he deserves.

Hit the Ground Running

To start something and proceed at a fast pace with enthusiasm. This expression can be used to refer to something in the past, present or future and can be used in reference to work or anything in life that has proceeded at a fast pace and with excitement.

Our new restaurant has really *hit the ground running*.

A: How's your new business going in social media marketing?

B: I am happy that it has really *hit the ground running*. I am operating at full capacity and will need to hire my first employee soon.

Down the Road

In the future. This can mean the near future or in the distant future. Either way, it refers to something we know will be coming.

This will need to be something we will focus on *down the road*.

A: I know you mentioned that there will be changes coming *down the road*, but I think we need to make those changes now.

B: I agree. I was thinking about this last week, and I was wrong to believe they could wait.

Call the Shots

Take the initiative in deciding how something should be done. We use *call the shots* to describe that we will make the decisions, especially for anyone who isn't capable of deciding on anything official.

Teachers *call the shots* in deciding how to teach children at school.

A: Who *calls the shots* at your house?

B: My dad definitely *calls the shots*.

Knuckle Down

Apply oneself seriously to a task. *To knuckle down* means that someone needs to become more serious about a specific task. Often college students need to *knuckle down* because there are many distractions at college. Also referred to as *buckle down*, which has the same meaning.

My mom told me to *knuckle down*, or I wasn't going to pass all of my courses this year and I think she's right.

A: We really *knuckled down* and completed everything before our deadline. That's fantastic.

B: Thank you for your help in making this happen.

Deep Dive/To Dive Deep

An in-depth examination or analysis of a topic. If we are looking to explore a topic in great detail, then we are doing a *deep dive*. *To dive deep* into a topic helps us understand it in great detail. Someone may ask you to *dive deep* into specific topics by examining them in detail.

Let's *dive deeper* into this area and find exactly what we need.

A: Is it necessary to do a *deep dive* for each area? We won't have much time to analyze this.

B: I understand, but it's the only way we can fully understand.

In the Same Boat

To be in the same difficult or unfortunate situation as others. We use, *in the same boat,* to explain that we are going through a similar situation as someone else.

We were both *in the same boat* and succeeded at providing the necessary information.

A: Have you spoken to Alice? She's *in the same boat* as you. Try reaching out to her and she could possibly give you some ideas.

B: I haven't spoken to her yet, but I will touch base with her today.

Take a Shot At (Something)

To take a shot at something is to try to do something. This expression is used in situations when there is a problem to be solved and we want to try and solve it. So, we *take a shot at it*. An example of *taking a shot at something* is if there was a hard calculus problem, and you decide you'll take a look and see if you can solve it.

She'd like to *take a shot* at basketball. Let her try it and see if she likes it.

A: Are you having trouble putting together that new bookshelf? Can I *take a shot at it?*

B: Sure, that'd be great. Thank you.

Have a Crack At (Something)

Make an attempt or have a turn at doing something. This expression is the same as *take a shot at something*.

Heather would like to *have a crack at it*, so let her try organizing the anniversary party.

A: I have been struggling putting up this playpen. Would you like to *have a crack at it?*

B: Please, I always lose my patience trying to put together furniture!

Game Plan

A strategy worked out in advance, especially in sports, politics, or business. We use *game plan* to stress that we have a plan in place and strategies for implementing our plan. This expression makes reference to sports, as teams that have a game plan win more games by following a strategy.

You don't need a *game plan* for every single aspect of your life. Sometimes it's fun to just go with the flow.

A: What is our *game plan*?

B: We'll need to focus more on customer retention and create strategies that will help us gain more customers.

Set the Pace

Lead the way in doing or achieving something. This may include speed, quality, or a level of standard that competitors may try to follow or emulate. Some major companies have *set the pace* in innovation and are ahead of all of their competition.

Space exploration has *set the pace* for new ways of traveling.

A: Our company has *set the pace* in our industry for all the advancements in technology and I wanted to thank everyone for all their hard work.

Exercise:

Use your new idioms to complete the phrases below.

1. Now we've reached the first milestone, we will _____ for the next quarter.

2. It's time for you to _____ and get some work done.

3. All of our children are the same age and genders, we're _____.

4. Sam wanted to _____ at the last meeting, but it didn't go well.

5. The new sales associate had record sales this week and _____ for the entire team.

6. I've never skied before, but I'd like to _____ and register for some lessons.

7. Let me _____. I may be able to figure out what keeps triggering our alarm.

8. We need a _____ for how we will secure employment after we graduate.

9. I'd like to get married _____ but not anytime in the near future.

10. We need to do a _____ into customer satisfaction.

11. I wish I could do something about this situation, but _____.

Answer Key:
(1) hit the ground running (2) knuckle down/buckle down (3) in the same boat (4) call the shots (5) set the pace (6) take a shot at it (7) have a crack at it (8) game plan (9) down the road (10) deep dive (11) my hands are tied

WORKPLACE IDIOMS AND EXPRESSIONS PART 10

Head Start

An advantage granted or achieved at the beginning of a race, a chase, or a competition. It's an early start before the official time to start something. Sometimes we try to give others a *head start* but in business you never want your competition to get a *head start* as this will cause a company to lose market share.

We need to get a *head start* on organizing our documents or we won't be ready for the deadline.

A: How were you able to complete everything by Friday?

B: I got a *head start* because I knew it'd take a lot of time and I wanted to complete it all.

Neck and Neck

Even in a race, competition, or comparison. We use this expression to explain that we are at the same spot as someone else or another company. We are *neck and neck* or in the same position to the extent that we are unable to tell who is better or winning.

We have been *neck and neck* with our competition for the last few years.

A: How was the hockey game last night?

B: It was great. Both teams were *neck and neck* the entire game, but the Toronto Maple Leafs scored in the last five minutes and won.

Hot on the Heels Of (Someone or Something)

Following close behind or soon after someone or something. If we are *hot on the heels of someone or something*, we are following right behind them. This may be an employee, co-worker, boss or competitor.

The cops are *hot on the heels* of those criminals.

A: Can you see which position we are in for Google Search?

B: Our competitors were *hot on our heels*, but we pulled away and took the top position.

Have a Lot of Time for (Someone)

To appreciate and respect someone. This expression shows that we vouch for someone within a business setting. We may express that we'd like a specific employee on our team, so we'd say that we *have a lot of time for them*.

We're looking to promote him, and everyone has said *they've got a lot of time for him*.

A: Who do you think we should choose for the new position in accounting?

B: *I have a lot of time for Oliver*; he really showed us his talent and works really hard.

Hear Me Out

To ask someone to listen to all of what we have to say, even reluctantly. We use *hear me out* to ask the other person to just listen and try to understand where we are coming from. Sometimes children will use this expression with their parents to try to get them to agree.

Please *hear me out* before you make a decision.

A: I would like to discuss this whole situation with you. Can you *hear me out?*

B: Yeah I will.

Stand Out

Attract attention by looking or behaving in a certain way that people may notice. We may also *stand out* by excelling at a certain skill that is above average. You might also hear *stand out from the crowd,* which has the same meaning.

His most recent work has really *stood out* from the previous work he has done.

A: We really need to *stand out* at the trade show. Any ideas for what we can do this year?

B: People are always interested in samples. If we get swag made up and sample products, then we will *stand out*.

Head (Somewhere)

To *head somewhere* is an informal verb meaning to leave, depart, or go. We can use *head* whenever we are leaving or departing a place.

You need to *head* home now. You haven't had a break all day.

A: Where are you *headed?*

B: I am going to the mall to buy a new outfit for the Christmas party tomorrow night.

Pull Some Strings

To use the power or influence one has over others to get what they want. They may be in a position of power and have the authority to influence other people's decisions. They often *pull some strings* to help someone else get what they want.

If you want to get this done faster, you might
need Peter to *pull some strings* for you.

A: I know you've been working with Microsoft for the last 10 years and I've just applied. Can you talk to HR and *pull some strings*?

B: I could do that for you.

All Hands on Deck

A situation in which every available person is needed or called to assist. We use *all hands on deck* to communicate that everyone must be involved and help with the work put before them.

The company needs an *all hands on deck* approach
to manage the most recent PR situation.

A: We require *all hands on deck* for upcoming months to reach our goals, would that be possible?

B: Absolutely, I will let my team and the other departments know we'll need their help.

If Need Be

If we want to indicate that something might become necessary, we use *if need be*. It is a way of saying that a certain action might be required, depending on certain other factors. Often, *if need be* is used to say to the listener that they can make a decision about particular details.

We've been waiting a long time, so we might have to leave without them *if need be*.

A: Can we cancel the New Year's party this year? Maybe we will have one the following year instead and travel to Italy to celebrate the new year.

B: *If need be*, but I really enjoy the New Year's party.

Pressing

Something that needs immediate attention and to be dealt with soon. If something is *pressing* it is urgent and to be focused on immediately.

We have a *pressing* business matter that needs to be taken care of before it becomes an even bigger problem.

A: There's been a *pressing* issue that needs to be addressed today. Can you be sure to focus mainly on this issue?

B: Absolutely, that'll be all we focus on until it's resolved.

Extra Practice - Exercise:

Now use the above expressions to fill in the blanks.

1. Let's _____ now. We've been at this restaurant for a couple hours already.

2. We need _____ in the next meeting.

3. If you'd just _____ then I can explain the situation to you more clearly.

4. The only way to _____ in your interview is to be different from the other applicants.

5. The election results were _____ .

6. We should be concerned our main competitor is _____.

7. I_____ for Rose and want her to apply to my team.

8. _____ we can raise our rates, but only if it's absolutely necessary.

9. We have a _____ issue with our suppliers; they continue to send defective products.

10. Can you _____ for my brother?

11. The other team got a _____ and began training months before us.

Answer key:

(1) head home (2) all-hands-on-deck (3) hear me out (4) stand out (5) neck and neck (6) hot on our heels (7) have a lot of time for (8) If need be (9) pressing (10) pull some strings (11) head start.

WORKPLACE IDIOMS AND EXPRESSIONS PART 11

Duck Your Responsibilities

To avoid or escape from an unpleasant task. We say that someone *ducks a duty or responsibility* when they avoid doing what needs to be done.

You're trying to *duck your responsibilities* and I won't allow it.

A: Some people try to *duck their responsibilities* and pass it along to others. How is that possible?

B: That's a great question since we're all aware.

Clear the Air

Defuse or clarify an angry, tense, or confused situation through discussion. We use *clear the air* to express that we would like to work through a situation that has been causing tension in hopes to reach an agreement.

Is now the right time to discuss some
pressing issues so we can *clear the air?*

A: Can we go chat? I really need to *clear the air.*

B: Yes, I'd really like that.

Painted with the Same Brush

To think that someone has the same bad qualities as another person because of how closely they worked together or for being in the same department. A similar phrase is *tarred with the same brush*. It refers to a situation where blame is given to multiple people or groups when that is not the case and one person should have been blamed.

Our department was *painted with the same brush* even though many of us work completely separately.

A: How was I *painted with the same brush* when I was just sitting in the corner staying quiet?

B: It's unfortunate, but everyone that was in the room was *painted with the same brush*.

Tactic

An action or strategy carefully planned to achieve a specific end. Sports games involve *tactics* to win. Companies use *tactics* as well to help promote and grow their business.

The company attempted to control the negotiation by using a delaying *tactic*, but it wasn't effective.

A: We will need to develop some *tactics* for the upcoming product promotions.

B: I agree. We should get all hands on deck to develop some new *tactics*.

Bury the Hatchet

To end a quarrel or conflict and become friendly. It is nice to *bury the hatchet* with anyone we still want to continue to have a relationship with. We are often required to *bury the hatchet* at work to keep amicable relationships. It can be difficult to *bury the hatchet*, but it is often of great benefit to develop this soft skill.

He can't *bury the hatchet*, and it looks really bad. If he could *bury the hatchet*, he'd be in a better place.

A: How were you able to *bury the hatchet?*

B: It wasn't easy, but with a lot of hard work, we were able to move past it.

Stick it to Someone

To intensely confront, punish, or retaliate against someone, perhaps vindictively or with unnecessary severity.

The reporters really *stuck it to him* during the press conference, not allowing him to evade any questions.

A: How did your conversation go?

B: Our boss really *stuck it to me*. I think I will have to go over everything and redo it.

Brought it on One's Self

Someone has caused something to happen to themselves. These are situations where we can't blame anyone but ourselves for what has happened. Whoever instigated the whole situation may have *brought it on*.

She was always complaining about her job to her boss and just got fired, so she really *brought this on herself*.

A: I have been arguing with my team a lot.

B: You really *brought it on yourself* by arguing with them and stubbornly ignoring your team's ideas.

Under the Gun

Under great pressure where timelines need to be met and there's a high level of stress. When we are *under the gun*, there is a lot of pressure to do something as quickly as possible. We may fear failing because of *pressing* timelines when we are *under the gun*. Within an organization, employees can be *under the gun* when there are tight or unrealistic deadlines.

Manufacturers are *under the gun* to provide replacement products after many defective products.

A: Hey Victoria, how's your day been going?

B: You know, it's been great, but I am *under the gun* trying to meet so many deadlines by month end that I'll need a nice vacation when I'm done.

Come up Empty

To be unsuccessful when trying to complete a task. We use *come up empty* to refer to the result of previous actions that have been unsuccessful.

We hired an outside recruiting company who has interviewed ten applicants who have all *come up empty*.

A: We tried to book a venue for our next event, but we *came up empty*. Any ideas?

B: Maybe we can change the date and see what's available for other days.

Extra Practice - Exercise:

Now use the above expressions to fill in the blanks.

1. Max has been _____ while working from home and was let go.
2. We need some well thought out _____ to help us negotiate.
3. Charlie has really tried to _____ but everyone has noticed.
4. Let's talk about what happen and hopefully this will _____.
5. During the press conference, the reporters really _____.
6. I'm sorry I have to fire you, James, but you really _____.
7. We really need to get these documents printed and work faster because we're really _____.
8. Just because the scandal involved our CEO, it's unfortunate that we all got _____ and it might be hard to find a new job.
9. It's time for you to _____ with your sister and stop all the fighting.
10. It's challenging looking for a new job; I always _____.

Answer key:

(1) slacking off (2) tactics (3) duck his responsibilities (4) clear the air (5) stuck it to me (6) brought it on yourself (7) under the gun (8) painted with the same brush (9) bury the hatchet (10) come up empty

WORKPLACE IDIOMS AND EXPRESSIONS PART 12

Blow the Whistle on Someone/Something

To tell the public or someone in authority about something wrong that you know someone is doing, especially in the workplace. This may be telling the authorities of dishonest or illegal behavior. A person who does this is called a whistle-blower.

The stock price plummeted after the employee *blew the whistle* on the corrupt financial reporting.

A: Did you read about the *whistler-blower* at Facebook who leaked tens of thousands of pages of internal documents that said Facebook put profit before user safety?

B: Yeah, that's crazy and the *whistler-blower* is going to testify and tell everything he knows.

Come to Light

Something that has become widely known. We use *come to light* when something has been revealed or exposed. If facts *come to light,* then they are known publicly. If information within a company comes to light, then it is new information that could sway decisions.

Discrepancies in the yearly budget report *came to light* after our accounting department analyzed them.

A: When did this *come to light*?

B: Well, it happened last week when you were on vacation.

Tally Up

To calculate the sum of something. We use *tally up* to say that we need to add everything up to find out how much we have.

Have we *tallied everything up* yet?

A: What is the total cost of owning a house in your city?

B: Well, if you *tally up* all the costs like mortgage, property taxes, insurance, and association fees, then it costs around $5000/month.

Take On

To agree to do something. If you *take on* new tasks, then you have decided to do it and have offered your help. We use *take on* to express that we are willing and able to do something.

I will *take on* the project if no one else is interested in doing it.

A: Who is the best fit to *take on* this role after he leaves?

B: Hmm, that's a really good question. Can I get back to you with that answer? I am just not sure if we have someone at the moment who can properly *take this on*.

Take Off

To suddenly start to be successful or popular. We use *take off* to express that someone or something has become successful in a short period of time. This can be a product, activity, career or business.

My overall health and fitness really *took off* after hiring a personal trainer and dietitian.

A: How did Ben's product *take off* on Amazon?

B: He found a program that taught him Amazon product marketing and from there applied what he learned and has been very successful.

Play-by-Play

A very detailed, thorough depiction of some event as each moment unfolded in real time. The term comes from sports, where a commentator might describe each part of the action in sequence, *play-by-play*.

You can just give me a quick rundown of how the meeting went; I don't need a play-by-play.

A: Can we speak so you can give me a play-by-play?

B: Yes, that needs to happen.

A Good Line of Sight

When a company has a *good line of sight* then there is a clear connection between the employee's goals and the organization's goals. There are many benefits to ensure that the employee's best efforts are helping to achieve the organization's goals. Another key element is that the employees know the work they're doing matters.

We must discuss these numbers with the finance team to get a *good line of sight*.

A: What needs to happen for us to get a *good line of sight?*

B: We need to stick to the plan that's in place and that time frame. Always changing the original work plan isn't giving us a *good line of sight*.

Roll Out

To officially launch or introduce something new, such as a product or service, especially for widespread sale to the public. We use *roll out* as an expression that explains that a company is making its new products or services available to the public.

A new marketing campaign is expected to *roll out* in the new year.

A: When will this new product *roll out*?

B: We will be *rolling it out* next month.

Precursor

A person or thing that comes before another of the same kind. The first thing often depends on the next to happen. In workflows, there are a number of *precursors* before we get to the final product. An example of a precursor is that dark clouds always come before a storm.

Taking time to meditate is a *precursor* to feeling calm and peaceful.

A: Is there a *precursor* that we are missing for this work?

B: I think we've covered all our bases, but as we move through each phase there may be some areas that need to be reworked.

Work out the Kinks

To try to fix the small problems or flaws. We can *work out the kinks* at work or in any type of situation where there may be small problems that need to be worked out.

We're still *working out the kinks* after installing the new software, but it will be ready by tomorrow.

A: How did your last conversation go?

B: Amazing, *we worked out all the kinks* and spoke for 3 hours.

On the Cusp

At the point when something is about to change into something else. We use *on the cusp* when we are close to achieving something that we set out to do and will change the future.

We are *on the cusp* of doing something great for this community.

A: We are *on the cusp* of a breakthrough. What can you add?

B: My team was vital in getting us to this point, and I really want to thank them for all their hard work.

Hiccup

When we have a small problem or difficulty. We use *hiccup* in situations that do not last very long or can be solved easily.

The recent sales *hiccup* is nothing to panic about. We are confident in what we need to do to fix this.

A: Is this just a *hiccup* or something more serious that I should be worried about?

B: Believe me, this is only a *hiccup*, and it'll be fixed soon.

Speed Bump

A speed bump is something that stops a person or thing from progressing. Within the workplace, there are speed bumps that occur and must be solved in order to move forward.

I don't want any *speed bumps* as this is the third time trying to make these changes.

A: Are there any *speed bumps* that may arise down the road?

B: No, we've tried to think of all possible scenarios, and there shouldn't be any *speed bumps* ahead of us.

Get Out of Something

To try to avoid or escape a duty or responsibility. We use *get out of something* when anyone tries to avoid doing what they have been assigned or asked and instead attempts to pass along the work to someone else. There are many situations where children try to *get out of doing* homework or cleaning their room.

The kiddos wanted to *get out of* folding the laundry.

A: How did you *get out* of doing that huge project?

B: I didn't want to *get out of* it. I was assigned to a bigger and more time consuming one.

Scale Back

Reduce something in size, number, or extent, especially by a constant proportion across the board.

Are there any other ways we can possibly *scale back*?

A: How do you see us *scaling back* on production costs in the coming months?

B: We need to focus on cost per unit. That's the only way for us to reduce costs.

Shadow

When new employees follow a more experienced employee to learn their new position. It is a form of training. The new employee acts like a shadow next to the person they are learning from, copying their actions so they better understand how to perform the job.

It's great to *shadow* a more experienced employee, but when we work from home, it's impossible.

A: Who will I *shadow* today?

B: You will *shadow* Joe today to learn how to use our client management system.

Extra Practice - Exercise:

Now use the above expressions to fill in the blanks.

1. I _____ a senior employee for a week and really *learned the ropes.*
2. I decided to _____ my work hours so I could spend more time with my kids.
3. I don't have a lot of time for a _____, I just need a quick overview.
4. We haven't _____ yet so it's been challenging.
5. The clothing startup really _____ during December.
6. Let's _____ the points from our game.
7. We had a few _____ but nothing major, and they were addressed quickly.
8. I need to _____ to the finance team to review.
9. We have a _____ going forward.
10. We will _____ the new plans in the new year.
11. Whenever an employee _____, they ruin their career.
12. Our business is _____ more than we can handle.
13. Graduating from high school is a _____ to going to college.
14. The power outage was a _____ in our operations today.
15. We are _____ of a great idea.
16. My sister always tries to _____ washing the dishes.

Answer key:

(1) shadowed (2) scale back (3) play-by-play (4) worked out the kinks (5) took off (6) tally up (7) hiccups (8) hand this on (9) good line of sight (10) roll out (11) blows the whistle (12) taking on (13) precursor (14) speed bump (15) on the cusp (16) get out of.

WORKPLACE IDIOMS AND EXPRESSIONS PART 13

To Go Against the Grain

To do something or be in opposition or contrary to what is generally understood, assumed, practiced or accepted.

The architect always tried *to go against the grain*, ignoring the popular trends of her day.

A: Sarah isn't afraid to *go against the grain* with her designs.

B: True and she's very good at it.

The Elephant in the Room

An obvious truth or fact, especially one regarded as embarrassing or undesirable, that is being intentionally ignored or left unaddressed.

We all sat sipping our coffee quietly, no one was going to bring up *the elephant in the room,* that David was laid off.

A: Why is everyone on edge?

B: No one wants to discuss the *elephant in the room*, that we may be shutting down.

That Ship has Sailed

One's opportunity (to do or achieve something) is no longer available or likely.

If you were hoping to ask Mia to go with you, *that ship has sailed*—she's going to the prom with Peter.

A: Hey, is that leadership position still open? My friend wants to apply.

B: No, that *ship has sailed.*

Turn a Blind Eye

To knowingly ignore some wrong-doing.

Can't you just *turn a blind eye* to this little incident, instead of telling my parents?

A: I know I made some mistakes in my work lately, but I need you to *turn a blind eye* just this once.

B: I am sorry I can't do that.

Off the Record

Not recorded for official publication; or, more informally, in confidence.

What I am about to tell you is *off the record*; the newspaper has decided to publish our article.

A: What happened at the party on Friday?

B: I can tell you, but this is *off the record!*

On the Record

Recorded for official publication; formally and publicly.

Please turn the cameras off—I don't want these comments *on the record*.

A: That former CEO had to go *on the record* for his deposition.

B: That's tough, but I think it's about time someone pushed him to tell the truth.

Make no Mistake

To say is something with absolute certainty; do not think otherwise.

Make no mistake, I intend to sue this company that breached their contract.

A: I am coming for your job, *make no mistake. Hehehe*

B: Go for it. I'm confident I'll be promoted soon anyhow and think you'll do great in this role.

When/If Push Comes to Shove

If the situation deteriorates or becomes desperate: if drastic measures are needed.

If *push comes to shove*, I will spend my extra savings to help out.

A: How can I recover the money we have lost?

B: If *push comes to shove,* we can sell one of our restaurants.

Champion Someone/Something

To fight for, defend, or support as much as possible.

We had everyone *champion* our cause to help children in need.

A: The company wants to take on a worthy cause for our community outreach.

B: I think we should team up with Habitat for Humanity. They're *championing* the affordable housing movement.

At the End of My Rope

Having reached a point of utter exhaustion or exasperation; in a state where one has no more patience, endurance or energy left.

The baby's been crying every night, and I haven't slept since she was born. I'm just *at the end of my rope*!

A: How can you work with him?

B: Honestly, I'm at *the end of my rope* with all his rude comments.

Drop It

Stop discussing this subject at once.

Yes, I was late again for lunch today, but can we *drop it* for now.

A: The boss never did anything to get our team on Campfire.

B: No, we're sticking with Trello. I think you'll have to *drop it*.

Extra Practice - Exercise:

Now use the above expressions to fill in the blanks.

Make no mistake _____
_____
_____

The elephant in the room _____
_____
_____

Turn a blind eye _____
_____
_____

That ship has sailed _____
_____
_____

On the record_____
_____
_____

WORKPLACE IDIOMS AND EXPRESSIONS PART 14

Go-Getter

A highly motivated and ambitious person.

We want to hire employees who are *go-getters*, not timid, indecisive people.

A: You're a real go-getter, whenever I mention any work that needs to be completed, you do it. Thank you.

B: You're welcome. Many times I've already started the work before you've even mentioned it though.

To Fly Blind

To do something based on guesswork, intuition, or without any help or instructions.

Since this is our first attempt at developing a startup, we'll be *flying blind* as we figure out what works best.

A: I don't have any background on the new client!

B: Neither do I. We'll have to *fly blind*.

To Catch (Someone) up on (Something)

To give someone the latest information on a particular topic or situation.

Anna *caught me up* already, so I know what to expect now.

A: I got stuck in traffic and missed the morning meeting. Can you *catch me up?*

B: Yes of course.

Got Your Back

To be willing and prepared to help or defend someone; to look out for someone in case they need assistance.

Don't worry about that meeting, I've *got your back* if any difficult conversations come up.

A: Can you help me approach the regional manager? I don't know why but he really intimidates me.

B: Don't worry, I *got your back.*

On the Books

Set down in writing or an audio or video recording.

Today is officially the coldest day *on the books.*

A: How did we do in sales last quarter?

B: Really well. Those were our highest numbers *on the books.*

Fair Shake

Just treatment; a fair chance to do something.

When Tara applied for her position, she was afraid she wasn't going to get a *fair shake* but that was not the case.

A: How do you know if you were given a fair shake?

B: You don't know, just try your best.

Run Something Past You

To explain or describe something to someone; to inform someone about something.

I have an idea I'd like to *run past you*. Do you have time today at 1pm?

A: What's your plan for the big presentation on Monday?

B: About that, could I *run something past you?* I have an idea but I'm not sure it will work.

Straight Shooter

A person who is honest and forthright.

You are a *straight shooter,* I always tell the truth about the situation, even if it's bad news.

A: Any advice on working with the guys from the regional office?

B: No, just be yourself. You're such a *straight shooter* I'm sure they'll love you.

Not on My Watch

That will not happen while I am in charge or on the lookout.

It *didn't* happen *on my watch,* the robbery took place 30 minutes after I left the store.

A: I hear the interns plan on throwing a party in the conference room Friday night after they finish taking inventory.

B: *Not on my watch!*

On a Whim

Based on a sudden, impulsive urge, desire or idea; without careful planning

On a whim, we drove to the beach for the weekend.

A: I don't think they planned on the long 3 day layover in New York.

B: But they got to explore the city.

Interested In (Phrasal Verb)

If you are *interested in* something, then you are absorbed in it and have a desire to want to learn more about it or spend more time doing it.

I am very *interested in* seeing the results from my exam after I studied so hard.

A: What are you *interested in*?

B: I like learning languages, snowboarding, reading and traveling. How about you?

A: I like any kind of art; painting, drawing, and sculpting are my favorites.

Wrap Up (Phrasal Verb)

To get to the point of what one is saying.

We need you to *wrap up*. You've been talking for nearly half an hour already and we're running short on time.

A: Sorry I am late, I had to wait for a conversation to *wrap up* before I could leave.

B: It's ok, I understand.

Exercise:

Write a sentence for each of this section's idioms. Ask a language partner to check your work.

Wrap up _____
_____
_____

Champion _____
_____
_____

Drop it _____
_____
_____

Run something past you_____
_____
_____

Straight-shooter _____
_____
_____

LANGUAGE FOR INTERVIEWS

Interviews are a unique linguistic challenge. Many interviewers ask the same questions, no matter the job although some enjoy asking out of the box questions. This section helps you practice some of the most common vocabulary and interview questions used for hiring.

Here are some words and phrases to practice when preparing for job interviews.

Tackle

Make determined efforts to deal with a problem or difficult task.

It's imperative to *tackle* the tough questions during a job interview. Prepare ahead of time for questions they will most likely ask.

A: I'd like to thank you for helping me *tackle* this massive project last week.

B: Oh you're welcome, let me know if you need any other help.

First Impression

How you are seen at the first meeting. A person's original opinion of you.

To make a good *first impression* at your interview, wear professional clothing, give a firm handshake and have a friendly demeanor with the interviewer.

A: The interview went really well, I got a really good *first impression*.

B: Oh great. *Impressions* are so important!

Research

An investigation or check into the history of something, like a business. You can research a thing, a time, a person, or an organization.

Be sure to do some *research* about the company before your interview to be better prepared and think of a few questions before you go in.

A: Are you familiar with our company culture?

B: Yes, and I was so impressed! Your philanthropy work is substantial.

Positive Personality Adjectives:

Adjectives you can use to describe yourself during a job interview.

Cooperative

Someone who works well with others to achieve a common goal.

I am very *cooperative* while working with others. I know that a successful business is almost always a team effort.

A: If you want to work here, you'll have to be comfortable in a *cooperative* setting.

B: That's how my last company worked as well. I'm much happier working with a team.

Diligent

To be careful with details, be on time, check to make sure all of your work is correct.

The lawyer was very *diligent* in preparing for his case in court.

A: I really need someone who has a high level of accuracy.

B: Well, I would say I'm quite *diligent* when it comes to my projects.

Prudent

Acting with or showing care and thought for the future.

She's a very *prudent* investor, always understanding the current situation before making any decisions.

A: Our clients want our advisors to be *prudent* with their accounts.

B: I assumed as much. I pride myself on being exceptionally *prudent*.

Versatile

Able to adapt or be adapted to many different functions or activities.

People are highly *versatile*, great at learning and naturally curious.

A: Our client list is quite varied, so you'll have to stay versatile to work here.

B: Oh, I see. I prefer to work with a wide range of clients.

Resourceful

Having the ability to find quick and clever ways to overcome difficulties with little resources.

She's a very *resourceful* person and is quick to react to any problem.

A: Our clinic has been very *resourceful* last month by shifting from hard copies to digital.

B: I couldn't agree more, we've saved so much time and money.

Meticulous

Showing great attention to detail; very careful and precise.

His work is always very *meticulous*, and we rarely find mistakes in the finished product.

A: Are you an organized person?

B: I'm beyond organized! I'm the most *meticulous* person I know.

Punctual

Happening or doing something at the agreed or proper time; on time.

Some cultures value being *punctual* while others don't seem to worry about *punctuality* at all.

A: It's important that you be *punctual* every day. We start our days with a quick, morning meeting.

B: I'm not concerned - I was always the first to arrive at my last office.

Ambitious

Having or showing a strong desire and determination to succeed.

He is very *ambitious* and woke up early each day but also worked long days.

A: What's a word you would use to describe yourself?

B: I guess you could say I'm very *ambitious*. I always see the opportunity to do something bigger and better.

Articulate

Someone who can clearly communicate their ideas fluently and coherently.

She is a very *articulate* and intelligent speaker so no one had any questions.

A: This is a law firm, so the boss is big on language. Can you *articulate* your message clearly?

B: Within my last role I was fortunate to practice my communications skills and learned how to *articulate* my message clearly.

Hands-On

Involving or offering active participation rather than theory.

He had a very *hands-on* training that helped him learn quickly.

A: Do you have any *hands-on* experience with this program?

B: No, but I've used several different programs that looked very similar to this one and I am sure I can learn it quickly.

Proactive

To anticipate and stop a problem before it happens. A policy, rule, or person can be proactive.

Sadie *proactively* anticipated and avoided any potential problems.

A: We don't want someone who only reacts. We prefer a more *proactive* approach.

B: I agree, that's the best way to do things.

Pragmatic

Dealing with things in a sensible, reasonable way based on experience and information.

Her English lessons are very *pragmatic*.

A: Would you describe yourself as a dreamer?

B: No, I'd say I'm quite *pragmatic*.

Dynamic

Someone who is positive in attitude and full of energy and new ideas.

We're looking for someone who is *dynamic* and determined.

A: How would you take a basic deck presentation and make it more dynamic?

B: I personally think a good deck doesn't need any sparkle - it speaks for itself.

Good at Reading People (Idiom)

When someone who is very perceptive and pays close attention to everything people say or do. If someone is *good at reading people*, they can understand subtle communication which may be words, body language, or expressions.

Our boss is really *good at reading people* and could tell I wanted to say something.

A: Would you say you're *good at reading people*?

B: I've really developed this skill in the last few years, I wasn't always *good at reading people* but now I can pick up on subtle cues.

Diplomatic

Having or showing an ability to deal with people politely. A leader who is diplomatic doesn't cause people to have bad feelings.

He is a very *diplomatic* leader because he chooses his words carefully.

A: How would you manage a difficult colleague who's resistant to change?

B: I'd find a kind, *diplomatic* approach to challenge my coworker with facts and numbers from the business.

Take Initiative

Someone who does things without being told.

Everyone is aware that he is great at knowing what to do and *taking initiative*.

A: Do you need a lot of direction at work or are you someone who *takes initiative*?

B: I prefer to *take initiative* by assessing the past day's work and then seeing where I can jump back in. I like staying on top of my work and not letting it fall behind.

TYPES OF SKILLS:

Below is a list of the different skills we need at work. Just like the ability to type and take notes in a meeting, we also need to work with people different from us, write clear emails and write up good reports. All of these skills fall into their own category:

Soft Skills

Personal attributes that enable someone to interact effectively and harmoniously with other people. There are many soft skills, but any skill that requires interacting in a productive way with someone else requires soft skills.

He's great with numbers, but I worry about Bob's *soft skills*.
He struggles to work with a team and he avoids his colleagues.

A: How much do you value *soft skills*?

B: Honestly, quite a bit. I've found that a team member with poor *soft skills* can really set back important work.

Communication Skills

A person's ability to convey information and ideas effectively.

I have improved my *communication skills* and also use a more friendly tone in every interaction.

A: Tell me about a time you used your *communication skills* to solve a problem at work.

B: One colleague of mine had trouble creating her own documents to track her workflow, so I made some templates for her to follow a consistent format and explained how to use them. Within 6 months her productivity drastically improved.

A Strong Work Ethic

A person's drive to do a good job and be a worthwhile employee. Often people with a *strong work ethic* are serious about work and go above and beyond.

We pay well at this company because we only hire devoted workers with a *strong work ethic.*

A: Do you have *a strong work ethic?*

B: Yes, both of my parents owned companies and had *a strong work ethic* that I have adopted and that they also taught me.

Teamwork Skills

How well you work in a team.

Teamwork skills are essential in this job. You'll have to make lots of group presentations to our clients.

A: How are your teamwork skills?

B: I designed a major piece of software with a large, international team last year, so I would say they're very good.

Ability to Take Initiative

You know what to do without being told.

Sam's *ability to take initiative* is a huge help and speeds up our progress.

A: What's your greatest strength?

B: I'd have to say it's my *ability to take initiative*. My past boss always praised me for getting started with little to no direction.

Analytical Skills

The ability to collect and analyze information, problem-solve and make decisions.

An architect needs good *analytical skills* to figure out how to build new energy efficient buildings.

A: How do you approach new clients in the initial phases?

B: I'm continually improving my *analytical skills* by collaborating with others. I bring in a teammate to join me in an initial assessment to better understand the problem we are solving for them.

Flexible

The ability to change to fit new circumstances.

Our clients often change their minds about what they want, so we need workers who are *flexible*.

A: What would you do if we had a major blackout and you couldn't work online?

B: I'd have to be *flexible* and organize everyone into analogue project teams.

Technical Skills

Technical skills are sets of abilities or knowledge used to perform practical tasks in the areas of science, the arts, technology, engineering and math. In most cases advanced technical skills require specialized training or education.

Can you tell me about any certifications you have for *technical skills* that could help you at work?

A: What else should I know about you?

B: I'm a big believer in continued education, specifically to build up my *technical skills*.

Organizational Skills

The ability to manage work, time, deadlines, goals and a number of areas in life effectively.

One of my biggest strengths is my *organizational skills*. I color-code everything and keep a hard and digital copy of all my past work.

A: What would you say is your greatest achievement?

B: I'm a big believer in having the most effective *organizational skills*. I attained 2 degrees while also working and I couldn't have done that if I wasn't organized.

INTERVIEW STYLES:

Open-Ended

Open-ended interview styles require the candidate to answer a series of questions. As such, the candidate is speaking for the majority of the interview. The candidate may talk about their skills or strengths, and experience that relate to their current role within their company.

Situational

In a situational interview, the candidate is required to use real-world examples of situations they experienced and explain how they solved problems. This is to show how the candidate handled these situations and would apply them to a possible role in the future.

Behavioral

Behavioral interview questions focus on the candidate's behavior in the past positions and what results and outcomes resulted from their actions. It is vital to use the STAR method for behavioral interviews. STAR stands for Situation, Task, Action, and Result. You must explain the *situation* that happened, the *tasks* you performed, the *actions* you took, and the *results* from those actions. This approach can help you highlight the skills that employers are looking for.

The interviewer may use a combination of styles during the interview. Being aware of the style of question will help you tailor your answer and to speak clearly and concise.

Top Interview Questions with Guided Answers:

- Tell me about yourself.
- Why should we hire you?
- What is your greatest strength?
- What is your greatest weakness?
- Why do you want to work for us?
- Why did you/why do you want to leave your last/current job?
- What is your greatest accomplishment?
- Describe a difficult work situation and what you did to overcome it?
- Where do you see yourself in five years?
- Do you have any questions for me (the interviewer)?

1. Tell Me About Yourself

- Keep your answer direct and to the point.
- Be work specific. Highlight where you are professionally. Explain what you have learned from past work experiences while discussing what makes you excited about this specific opportunity.
- Research the company's values and what they are looking for in their employees and try to show the hiring manager that you possess these qualities.
- Don't dive into your whole life story.
- Don't discuss your experience that isn't related to the job.

Example - I went to university in Houston where I studied finance. After school I got my first job working for an oil and gas company. I wanted to expand my skills, so I took an MBA course and started networking with others in my field. That's how I found out about the open position here - my friend Maria told me about it.

2. Why Should We Hire You?

This is another very common question asked during an interview and can really help you stand out if your answer demonstrates that you're a good fit for the company. The key is to be specific. Before the interview, research what the company needs and how you will help them. Understand why they're looking for someone and some possible problems the new hire may have to solve. The more you can show how you will solve these problems, the more suitable you are for the position.

- Show that you are suited for the position and will solve their problems.
- Demonstrate that you have researched the company and know specific details about what they are looking for.
- Tell a story that highlights a time where you solved a specific problem and that you have the qualities they want.
- Don't be too modest—or too arrogant! There needs to be a balance between showing your skills but not being too over-confident.
- Make sure to answer why you're a perfect fit for this position. Don't talk about why you want this role.

Example - I believe I am a good match for this position. I am skilled and have experience in various areas that this position needs. For example, my current role manages 2 major facilities financial statements, I would then apply those same skills but at a larger scale within your organization.

3. What Is Your Greatest Strength?

This is really your time to shine.

- Talk about a strength that is directly related to the position you are applying for.
- Be sure to have a few answers ready because the hiring manager may ask you for more than one strength.
- In your research on the company and the job description, find out what strengths the company emphasizes most.
- Only make claims about yourself that you can back up with stories and examples.
- Only focus on your strengths that are relevant to the role.
- Be honest about your strengths. Don't oversell yourself, as if they hire you, you will underperform.

Example: I have to say that my greatest strength is my ability to coordinate people. I really like finding out who has what ability, how to organize who does what, and assign tasks to each person's strengths.

4. What Is Your Greatest Weakness?

This question is difficult to answer, but with the right preparation, you can give an awesome answer that will make you stand out.

- Let the hiring manager know that you are aware of the weakness described in your answer and that you have taken steps to overcome it.
- You can even go a step further to provide examples of something you've done to overcome this weakness.
- Make sure you are honest with your answer. Don't just google the best answer and copy what it suggests. The hiring manager can see right through these answers because they've heard them way too much.

- Avoid bringing up a weakness that is core to the job. Use an example of a weakness that won't affect your day-to-day work if they hire you.
- Make sure you answer this question. Providing a vague, indirect response is not what they're looking for.

Example - I know I'm not the most organized person, so I deal with it ahead of time. I make sure to set up my desk first thing in the morning and before I go home in the evening so that nothing gets lost or overlooked. I am working at improving it, but I know something essential could get buried under a pile of papers.

5. Why Do You Want to Work for Us?

The hiring manager wants to know what your motivation is for working for them. Is it just for money? Or will you commit to the company and grow with it?

- It's critical that you communicate to them that your wants coincide with their needs.
- Discuss specific things you like about the company and compliment them on something they've been recognized for recently.
- Never give them the impression that you won't stay with the company for a long time or that you just need a job and money. From their perspective, these are terrible reasons that should be kept to yourself.

Example - I really feel we're a good fit for one another. I've pushed myself to grow as a real estate agent, built up my skills, and built great relationships with all my past clients. I want a new challenge and I believe this is the best place for me to find it.

6. Why Did You/Why Do You Want to Leave Your Last/Current Job?

This can be a bit of a nerve-racking question if you left your previous job on bad terms. If you were fired, for example, then you need to own up to it. Describe what you have learned from the experience and steps you've taken to address the mistakes you made. Never conceal this information, but instead let them know of the situation and how you have learned from it.

- If you left voluntarily, then also let them know the reason. Be honest but never insult your previous company, bosses, or colleagues. You may have left simply because the work wasn't challenging enough and there were no opportunities for advancements. Keep your answer simple but direct.

- Avoid comparing the current company with your previous one. Try focusing on the question that's been asked about your previous company.

- There is some vocabulary, such as "downsizing," "budget cuts," and "recession" that are often used as reasonable reasons for leaving a job that the hiring manager will understand. If these are true, use them to describe your situation.

Example - Unfortunately, my last company experienced some financial troubles. They had to downsize and make some big cuts to the budget. My job and a lot of others were lost to save the company. I understood that they no longer needed my position and began to look for another job.

7. What is Your Greatest Accomplishment?

This question is similar to your greatest strength, and you can follow a similar format with answering it.

Pick an accomplishment that you know the company values and highlight the qualities you have that fit with this position.

If you have several accomplishments, that's great, but now is not the time to discuss all of them. Select one. Choose the one that has the most impact and that aligns most with the role you're interviewing for.

When discussing your accomplishment, show passion. The more passionate you are about your accomplishments, the more your personality and drive in life will shine through.

Never undermine your accomplishments. Any accomplishment that aligns with the company values will show the interviewer your skills for the position.

Example - I'm so proud to be the recipient of the Golden Pencil, an advertising award. I was part of a team that made an ad that not only got a ton of air time on network TV but also got viewed online over three million times. I helped come up with the concept and I developed the script.

8. Describe a Difficult Work Situation and What You Did to Overcome It.

This is one of the most common behavioral interview questions and the most troublesome. You will need to have a story of success ready to go for this question. Once again, choose a situation where you need to use skills specific to the job you're being interviewed for.

- Make sure you're specific and concise with your answer. Use the STAR (Situation, Task, Action, Result) method in answering this question.
- Avoid insulting previous co-workers, bosses, or companies when describing your accomplishments.

- Be direct and to the point. Rambling is not recommended for any question but when we begin to speak about ourselves, it is easy to ramble so take care to avoid this.

Example - I had a minor issue at my last job. I worked with a fellow creative, and we couldn't seem to see eye to eye. Every time we got a new assignment it seemed to lead to some tension. She didn't like my work style, I wanted to throw out all of her ideas, and on and on. Then one day I realized something, after our sessions of disagreement we always ended up finding a great idea. Eventually, we had to accept this as part of our process. If we let ourselves be direct, we eventually landed on an idea our boss loved.

9. Where Do You See Yourself in Five Years?

This seems like a very simple, straight forward question but when you dig deeper, it isn't, and you might get caught in a couple of traps.

- First, let them know the level of commitment you have to the position they are interviewing you for.
- Next, demonstrate how you are looking to grow and provide a realistic picture of how that will occur. This needs to align directly with the role you're applying to.
- Stress the importance of a long-term commitment with the company.
- Make sure that your answer is realistic and not something that is too far from reality.
- Never compare yourself to anyone within the organization. And never say that you want to take their position as CEO, HR Manager, etc. You will only shoot yourself in the foot!

Example - In five years, I'd like to have more experience in video ads. I already have quite a bit, but the competition for video and the audience's attention is always tough. And I think a lot of new changes are coming to audio and video. I hope to be in a higher position, perhaps eventually managing a department.

10. Do You Have Any Questions for Me (the interviewer)?

Have questions ready. Never say that you don't have any questions, it looks bad and unprepared.

- Ask questions you have regarding the company and what exactly you can do for them.
- It's always a best practice to mention something that you discovered in your research and need more clarity on. But be careful not to ask for information that can be found on the company's website.
- Be clear that you are focusing on what you can do for them and not just on yourself.
- Try not to ask any questions about benefits, vacations, salary, or anything that hasn't been brought up by them and can be a sensitive topic.
- Furthermore, don't ask about advancing to new roles. Just focus on this position.

Example - Yes, I do. Could you please walk me through what a day in this role would look like?

Yes, I need to know more about your company's culture. How would you describe it?

Some more tips:

- Consider hiring a skilled interviewer to help you prepare for your interview.
- Be your authentic self, don't try to be someone you aren't and definitely don't claim to have skills you don't.
- Avoid common pitfalls, such as inappropriate body language, talking too much, or using a cell phone.
- *Follow up* with the interviewer afterwards. Send a quick email to the interviewer if you haven't heard back from the company. Make sure to thank the company in your email.
- If you didn't get hired, find out why and use this knowledge for your next interview.

Practice Interview Dialogue:

Read through this conversation with a language partner to practice before your big interview. Take turns being the interviewer and the applicant.

Interview: Hello! Have a seat. I'm so glad you could join me today.

Applicant: Thanks so much for meeting me. I'm really excited about this job.

I: That's great to hear. Can you tell me a little bit about yourself?

A: Certainly. I grew up in New York and I studied accounting. Then, I moved around America where I got a master's in Washington, D.C. I got my first job at the KPMG. I really enjoyed tackling the opportunity to get the organization involved in more updated accounting software. Now, I'm hoping to move into the nonprofit sector.

I: Great! That all sounds lovely. I don't know much about New York myself, but I hope if you come to work here you can teach me a bit.

A: I hope so, too! I love to talk about my home country. But, I'm here to help promote your organization.

I: Yes, I have some questions for you. First, are you familiar with Trello, Campfire, and ClickUp?

A: Yes, I am well-versed in all of those platforms.

I: Great. Are you okay with working remotely? We only use the office for big meetings or presentations. Otherwise, you'll be online.

A: Sure thing. I feel comfortable collaborating online with my co-workers. I pride myself on my chat and email skills.

I: Can you tell me about your biggest accomplishment?

A: Well, I would have to say my biggest accomplishment was a presentation I organized in honor of Hung King Festival, a celebration of our ancestors. My team and I built a temporary shrine and organized volunteers to make a mini pilgrimage. We had to create the show and then promote it to the surrounding community. Together, we made a social media campaign, a promotional website, and a TV ad. The campaign and the event were a huge success.

I: Were you the project manager for that one?

A: Actually, I split the role of Project Manager with one of my seniors. We had a lot to manage and it made sense to divide up the work.

I: What would you say is your biggest weakness?

A: I struggle to leave anything unfinished at the end of the day. I know it sounds like I'm bragging, but it really does drag me down. Instead of clocking out at the end of the day, I tend to stay behind and keep working. I'm trying to stop so I can balance out my personal time with work.

I: What about your biggest strength?

A: I think my biggest strength is my ability to read people. I can see when someone is upset or has an issue with someone else long before my colleagues notice.

I: Great. Well, that's all my questions. Do you have any questions for me?

A: Yes. I wanted to ask about this position. It appears to be a new position in your company, is that correct?

I: That's right. We're taking on more clients and that means we need a whole department dedicated to marketing. Before, we did it all ourselves, just on the side of our normal duties, but that's no longer working.

A: Okay. With that in mind, can you tell me what you want to see in your new marketing department?

I: Oh, good question! I guess I want to see a dynamic group of co-operative, creative people ready to take on any challenge. It will be demanding - anyone who comes to work with us will have to be flexible and able to work on a budget. Does that sound like something you want to do?

A: Yes, very much! I hope I can be an asset to your company.

I: Well, I can't say anything yet, but I have a very good feeling! We'll follow up with you within the week to let you know if we'd like to see you again.

A: Thank you so much. And thank you for your time today. I really appreciate it.

I: Great to meet you! I hope to see you again soon.

KEY EMAIL VOCABULARY AND EXPRESSIONS

Email writing is a key skill. You never want to come across as rude or inconsiderate in any emails, so make sure you know how and when to use each expression. At the end of the section, you have some practice emails to help you prepare before you send an email.

Look Forward To

To feel happy and excited about something that is going to happen. We need to know and use this expression in meetings, emails, conversations, and at any point we feel excited. This is a very common and widely used expression that shows we are excited about meeting someone or future work that may be coming. Any area of life or work that we are excited about is something to *look forward to*.

I *look forward to* meeting you.

A: Thank you for the invitation, I am really *looking forward to* dinner on Saturday night.

B: We are also *looking forward t*o it. See you on Saturday.

To Take (Something) into Consideration

To think about something before making a decision, we use *to take something into consideration* to let the other person know that we need more time to think about it and that we are aware.

We will *take your experience into consideration* before choosing a candidate.

A: What do we still need *to take into consideration* for our upcoming event?

B: We have finalized everything except one last detail regarding the gifts, but that should be taken care of today.

To Follow Up

Pursue or investigate something further. We may gather more information, or we may need to reinforce or evaluate a previous action. We *follow up* on something in the near future to focus on something current that needs to be addressed.

I'd like to *follow up* with you in a week to discuss this project further.

A: Were you able to *follow up* with Ryan this afternoon?

B: I was, and everything looks great and is ready to go.

To Touch Base/Get in Touch

To briefly make contact with someone. We *touch base* with someone by communicating with them briefly through a message, phone call, or a quick stop by their desk.

I *touch base* with my boss every Monday at 9am.

A: Were you able to *touch base* with your vendor this morning?

B: We did have a quick meeting to discuss last week's event, and everything went well.

Don't Hesitate/Feel Free

Don't hesitate means to not pause or stop to do something. *Feel free* means to not hesitate before doing something. *Feel free* and *don't hesitate* have the same meaning, but *feel free* is more informal while *don't hesitate* is more formal.

Please *don't hesitate* to call or email me with any questions.
Feel free to email me anytime.

A: *Feel free* to reach out to me with any further questions you may have.

B: Thank you, I really appreciate the offer. I *won't hesitate* to reach out.

Interested In

If you are *interested in* something, then you are absorbed in it and have a desire to want to learn more about it or spend more time doing it.

I am very *interested in* learning Business English,
I've actually never studied it before.

A: Are you *interested in* learning how to code? I can teach you.

B: That sounds amazing, let's plan that. Thank you!

Forward

To send an email on to a further destination. When we receive an email, we can then *forward* that message on to someone else.

I have *forwarded* this email *on* to my team.

A: Have you *forwarded* me the new job posting description?

B: I've just completed it and will forward it to you now.

Attach

To add a document or file to an email. We *attach* documents to an email.

I have *attached* a copy of the contract for you to review.

A: Please send the *attachment*, I didn't receive it in the previous email.

B: Sorry, I forgot to *attach* it to my last message.

Reply

Write an email back to someone. Whenever we are responding to someone through an email, then we are *replying*.

Have you had a chance to *reply* to our suppliers?

A: Thanks for reaching out to me. Please forgive the late *reply*.

B: I understand, you've probably had many emails.

To Copy/Carbon Copy (CC)

Adding other recipients to the email to keep them informed.

I've *copied* Joe on this email, so he will know what we're planning.

A: Could you please make sure to CC the boss on any communications?

B: Sure, I'll *copy her in on* these messages.

Blind Carbon Copy (BCC)

An email message that is sent out without the group's awareness of its recipients. For example, you might send a BCC to your boss to show them the status of a project or to ask for clarification about something a colleague has mentioned.

Any official complaints need to be *BCC'd* to HR and the CEO.

A: I don't want to get everyone upset, so I sent a copy of this email to management as a *BCC*.

EMAIL STRUCTURE AND CONTENT

A formal, work email has an expected structure. When you don't follow it, you can come across as unprofessional or inattentive. However, writing an informal email to a friend or colleague who already knows you and your sense of humor can be much more casual.

It's also important to use the correct words, as we practiced earlier. The vocabulary used depends on whether it's a formal or informal email.

Greetings – If a message is formal, and the person is someone you don't know well, use a title—e.g., Mr/Mrs/Miss/Dr—and their last name. If a message is informal, and the person is someone you have been in communication with for a while, use their first name or a group greeting.

Closing – For a formal email use one these: Respectfully yours, Sincerely, or Best Regards, Kind Wishes, Warm regards, Warmest regards, With warm regards, Thank you.

Could is used to ask a polite question or to suggest a solution.

Could you please make some time for a meeting on Monday?

A: I think we *could* try it Mary's way. She has good ideas.

Contractions (*I'm, you're, won't,* etc.) are used less often in formal language. Formal language uses full forms (*I am, you are, will not,* etc.).

Phrasal Verbs are common two or three-word phrases that are used at work. Here are four common phrasal verbs used in emails.

Kick Off - To start something new like a project or a big change in the company.

Buckle Down - To work hard and not stop until something is ready or complete.

Hit (Someone) Up - To ask for help or request something from someone.

Wrap Up - To complete a project, meeting, or presentation.

Formal Email Examples:

Dear Mr Davies,

I **apologize** for the late reply. We have been **renovating** our office this week. The work should **wrap up** on Monday.

I am delighted **to inform** you that your application for a grant has been approved. **Please find the attached agreement.**

Could you please visit our office tomorrow so that we can sign the paperwork? I'm leaving the office at 5pm so please try to arrive before then. Please bring with you **all relevant company documents.**

Kind Regards,
Sally

More Formal Email Examples:

Dear Mr. Jones,

We **received** your delivery this morning and **noticed** that some of the goods were damaged. **Since this is not** the first time that this has happened, my boss is considering changing suppliers.

I look forward to your reply.

Regards,
Jane Roberts

Dear Mr. Brown,

Thank you for your **interest in** our product range. **Please find attached** the information you **requested**. If you **require** any further information, please **do not hesitate** to contact me.

Best Regards,
Deacon Smith

Informal Email Examples:

Hi Chris,

I'm sorry but I can't **make it** on Friday. Can we **put the meeting off** until tomorrow? Let me know if that'll work for you.

Regards,
Kelly

Hello,

I **found your advertisement** in a recent edition of The Entrepreneur. I would be grateful if you could **send me** some information about your company's product range.

Thanks in advance,
Joseph

Hello Jack,

We are **reaching out** to you because we have seen from our records that you have not paid your last invoice. **Could you** transfer the outstanding amount as soon as possible?

Best Regards,
Liam Jones

Hi Mia,

Thank you for all your help. Our team found the conference very useful. Do **get in touch** next time you are in our area.

Regards,
Michael

Practice: Now use the above expressions to fill in the blanks.

(a) _____ Ms Smith,

In reference to your job advertisement on LinkedIn, I wish to (b) _____ for the English teacher position at your school. (c)_____, please find my cover letter and resume for your (d) _____.

(e)_____,

Rob John

Answer key:

(a)Dear (b) apply (c) attached (d) consideration (e) Best Regard

(a) _____ Nicole,

I am very sorry to hear about the current problems your company is experiencing. We have had a problem with one of our current suppliers. We have (b) _____ and have replaced them this month. I assure you that the problem has been resolved and this will not happen again. We will send your products immediately.

If I can be of any further assistance, please (c) _____ to(d) _____ me _____.

Best Regards,

Matthew Jones

Answer key:

(a) Dear (b) taken this into consideration (c) do not hesitate (d)hit me up.

Extra Credit:

1. Here are some more informal expressions:

2. It looks like we really need to <u>redo</u> (renovate) the office.

3. Shelley <u>is off</u> (on vacation) at the end of the month.

4. Don't worry. I'll <u>back you up</u> (support you) during the meeting.

5. Good news, it looks like our application finally <u>went through</u> (got to the recipient).

6. If sales keep dropping, we are very likely to <u>go under</u> (fail or go bankrupt).

7. I haven't <u>gotten around</u> (found the time) to contacting the client yet. I'll do it first thing tomorrow.

8. I tried to call him several times, but I couldn't <u>get through</u> (make contact).

9. I'm afraid I have to <u>call off</u> (cancel) tomorrow's meeting.

KEY PHONE CONVERSATION IDIOMS AND PHRASES

When we speak English on the phone, we use many idioms and phrases that we don't use in any other situation. This can make talking on the phone very challenging, especially if you hear many different accents. If you need to improve your phone conversation skills, then this section will help you and please apply what you've learned as soon as possible. Let's get started.

In the Office - At work in a specific room or department.

Right now Mark is *in the office* attached to his house.

A: Can I speak to Jenny?

B: No, sorry. She's not *in the office.*

At the Office - At work in a typical office.

Maria isn't home, she's *at the office*.

A: Where are you right now?

B: I'm *at the office* so I'll have to call you back.

Out of the Office - Gone for the day or a period of time.

We can't talk to the boss today, she's *out of the office*.

A: Do you have any openings this week?

B: Sorry, half of our staff is *out of the office* until the 15th.

Out at the Moment - Stepped out or left for a brief period of time.

Brenda is *out at the moment*. She's picking up lunch for her team.

A: Hey, where did Brad go?

B: He's *out at the moment*.

Put Through - Connecting a call between two people.

Could you *please put me through* to your HR department?

A: Hi, I need to speak to someone in finance.

B: One moment, I'll put you through.

Catch What (Someone) Said

This expression means to hear and understand what someone has said. It is mostly used for questions and negative sentences.

I am sorry, could you repeat that? *I didn't catch what you said.*

A: That boy was very cheeky.

B: What was that? I didn't *catch what you said*.

Spelling Over the Phone

Whenever you need to spell out your name, the name of your business, or any other word with a difficult spelling, you'll have to use a special system.

For example, if you wanted to clarify the law firm Dalton, Fisch, and Hightower, you would need to clarify their spelling. Certain letters are easy to understand, but there are many that sound the same.

A: Could you please spell Fisch for me?

B: Certainly. It's F as in Fred, I, S as in Sam, C as in Charlie, and H.

Hang Up

On the telephone, if somebody *hangs up* this means that they have ended the call and are no longer available to speak.

She *hung up* the phone on me because it was a poor connection.

A: Could you please hand the phone to Mike?

B: I'll have to find him. Stay on the line - don't *hang up*.

Call You Back

To call (someone or someplace) on the telephone again, usually after failing to reach the desired person the first time.

I will *call you back* on Monday at 5pm. Hopefully, you're available at that time.

A: Hi, is the boss in?

B: Yes, but he's in a meeting. He'll have to *call you back*.

Hold On/On Hold

To ask someone to wait for a short period of time is to ask them to *hold on*. This is also similar to *put you on hold*, or to pause the phone call for a moment.

Please *hold on* and I will get you the information you need.
I need to put you *on hold* for a moment. Please don't hang up.

A: Is anyone in marketing available to talk to me?

B: Perhaps. Can I put you *on hold* while I check?

Cut Off

A pause in the phone connection that interrupts the conversation.

Hi, this is Will, I am calling you back, we must have gotten *cut off*.

A: Thanks for calling me back.

B: We drove through a tunnel and our call *got cut off*.

Get Through

To succeed in connecting with someone on the phone.

Were you able to *get through* to the cable company today?

A: We really need to talk to the internet company.

B: I tried to call them yesterday, but I couldn't *get through*.

Turn/Switch Off

Within a workplace, we use turn off for telephone, audio, or web calls to instruct people about what to do with a device.

For our video conference today, please *switch off* the audio unless you're speaking.

A: Before we start the meeting, everyone please *switch off* your phones so we have no interruptions.

Practice

Read through this dialogue with a partner to practice your phone idioms.

Receptionist: Hello, you've reached the offices of Beller and Beller. How can I help you?

Caller: Hi. I'm trying to reach Brenda in accounting. Is she in her office?

R: Oh, I'm sorry, she's out of the office. She'll be back on Tuesday. Can I take a message?

C: Sure. This is Diane Bell calling from the office of Long Horn Engineering. I need to follow up on an invoice.

R: Could you spell your name for me?

C: Of course. It's Diane - D as in delta, I, A, N as in night, and E as in echo.

R: Thank you for that. Oh, you know what, I think Brenda's assistant just walked in. Could you hold on a moment?

C: Yes, of course.

R: Okay, I'm putting you on hold. Please don't hang up. (pause) Hi, are you still there?

C: Yes, I'm here.

R: I'm transferring you to Brenda's office now. Have a good day.

C: You too!

MEETING PHRASAL VERBS AND IDIOMS

Idioms help English speakers communicate at work, but these expressions can be confusing to anyone who doesn't grow up hearing them on a regular basis.

Here are some of the most common idioms for you to practice.

Run Through Something - to look at or examine a set of things.

We *ran through* the list of applicants and there are a few qualified candidates.

A: I'd like to *run through* something with you. Do you have any time this week?

B: I have a lot of time tomorrow, you can take a look at my calendar and book some time.

Took Place - happened.

The interview *took place* on Monday and it went really well.

A: When will we have the opening ceremonies for the upcoming event?

B: The opening ceremonies will *take place* on June 1st.

Take Over - assume control of something.

IT Electronics completely restructured the company when they *took over*.

A: When will the new manager start?
B: She'll *take over* next month.

Go Over - consider, examine, or check something.

I'd like to *go over* our plans with you again.

A: Let's *go over* the presentation one last time tomorrow.
B: That'll be great.

Move On - to start doing something new or making progress.

I've been with this company for 20 years,
so it's time for me to *move on*.

A: We will *move on* to discussing the merger. Does anyone have any objections?
B: No, we are all looking forward to it.

To Reach Out to Someone - to offer help or support to someone.

Please *reach out to me* if you have any questions.

A: Have *we reached out to* the psychologist yet?
B: No, we will contact her today.

To Break Up - to break into pieces.

The conference *broke up* at 12pm. We'll reconvene at 1pm after lunch.

A: Would it work if we *break up* the next section into 2 groups?
B: That is exactly what I was thinking.

To Run Out of Something - to use up, not have anything left.

We are about to *run out of time*, let's call it a day and meet back up tomorrow first thing in the morning.

A: I've *run out of paper* for the printer, do you know where I might find some more?

B: Yah of course, it's over here in this drawer.

Deal With

When you *deal with* someone or something, you give your attention to it, often solving problems or making a decision concerning them.

I am busy *dealing with* a situation we are having at work, so I will be home late.

A: How do you want to *deal with* this situation?

B: Let me think about it for the rest of the day and get back to you tomorrow.

Come Back To or To Park Something

to not deal with something or answer a question immediately but leave it for a later time.

I'd like to *come back to* this topic later today.

A: Can we *park* that idea until our next meeting?

B: Definitely.

Close – to end

Let's discuss one last topic before we *close*.

A: Before we *close* for the day, are there any other questions or comments?

B: Nope, we are good.

To Preside Over

to be in charge of something while important things or decisions are happening.

The government *presided over* the educational changes.

A: Do we have someone to *preside over* our annual meeting?

B: Yes, we have the head of HR taking care of that.

Agenda

a list of items to be discussed at a formal meeting.

We have a lot on our *agenda*, so let's get this meeting started.

A: Can we *park* that idea until our next meeting?

B: Definitely.

Item – one part of a list.

Item six - we need to discuss the new client's concerns.

A: How many more *items* do we need to address?

B: There are three left. .

Input

something that is put in, such as a comment, advice, or opinion.

Linda, can I get your *input* on the new shoe ad layout?

A: Do we need any other unbiased *input*?

B: Definitely.

Brainstorming

group discussion to produce ideas or solve problems.

Brainstorming can generate some wonderful ideas.

A Let's put together a new group to *brainstorm* some more ideas.

B: That'd be great.

Absentee

a person who is expected or required to be present at a place or event but is not.

There are several *absences* from school this week because of the flu.

A: Did everyone show up?

B: There were four noticeable *absentees* yesterday.

Chairperson

The chairperson of a meeting, committee, or organization is the person in charge of it.

Carl, I know you love to organize events, so I'm making you *chairperson* of the party committee for the office.

A: Who is the *chairperson* for our upcoming meeting?

B: That'll be Lucy.

Clarification

the action of making a statement or situation less confused and more comprehensible.

Please advise us if you require further *clarification*.

A: Who can I speak to to get *clarification*?

B: I can help you with that.

Consensus

a general agreement among a group of people.

The *consensus* of the group was to meet everyone Monday morning.

A: Are we all aligned and have come to a *consensus*?

B: Yes we have.

Objective

a thing aimed at or sought; a goal.

The system has achieved its *objective*.

A: Have we reached the overall *objective* for this research?

B: Not yet but hopefully soon.

Show of Hands

A vote where a group of people will raise their hands to show whether they are for or against something; this is often used as an estimate of the numbers for or against each side.

Let's have a *show of hands* to see where everyone stands.

A: Can we see a *show of hands* for everyone in agreement with the changes?

B: I agree with them.

Compromise

A deal or agreement made between two parties where each party gives up a part of their demand.

That was a great *compromise,* and everyone walked away happy.

A: I know we aren't in agreement but can we make some sort of *compromise*?

B: I am willing to *compromise*.

Win-Win Situation

Each party will benefit in some way.

This deal has worked out for everyone! It's a *win-win situation*.

A: Can we think of a *win-win situation*? At the moment it doesn't seem as though we will receive much in this deal.

B: I'd like to work out a plan with you.

Meet Halfway

To give a little in return for something else or a compromise.

I know you want to be Project Manager, but I have more experience with this client. Can you *meet me halfway* and share the project with me?

A: Can we *meet the contractors halfway* with price?

B: We can always try.

In Writing

To write something in order to make it official and to serve as a document or proof of the conversation.

The rental lease needs to be *in writing*.

A: Could we get this *in writing*?

B: Yes, I'll make that happen.

Get Sidetracked

A distracted

I often *get sidetracked* when I am trying to work and someone is talking. I find it challenging to concentrate.

A: I understand everyone's concerns, Let's not *get sidetracked*. We were discussing the new position that will be opening. Can we think of any great candidates?

B: I agree with them.

Anything to Add

When there may be more to say about a topic before closing a meeting or changing to a new topic. This is everyone's last opportunity to speak up on a specific subject at a meeting.

I've said everything I needed to and don't have *anything to add*.

A: Before we wrap up, does anyone have *anything to add*?

B: No, no one has *anything to add*.

Exercise: Matching

Directions: Match the idiom to the explanation. For example: A question to see if anyone has any final thoughts ---- Anything to add.

1. A moment when both sides
   get what they want   a. brainstorming
2. The majority of opinions   b. input
3. One of the things on the agenda   c. move on
4. A group of people listing out ideas   d. win-win
5. To leave behind something
   familiar and try something new   e. consensus
6. To summarize something from
   a past meeting or project   f. compromise
7. An agreement in which each side
   gives up something   g. item
8. to help solve a problem   h. input
9. A person's opinion

KEY VOCABULARY FOR PRESENTATIONS

This section focuses on words you can use in a presentation. This set of vocabulary is more formal and technical to help you impress your audience while staying professional. Presentations are great language practice - be sure to get up there and rule the conference room!

We'll start with some positive words to use when you want to show that something is going well.

Trends – a general direction in which something is developing or changing.

This year we expect to see more home gym sales thanks to the current *trend* of working out with an online studio.

Rise - to go up, either literally or symbolically.

Our sales *rose* after the first quarter.

Grow – To build on what you already have.

The product sales *grew* substantially this past quarter.

Growth – The evidence of progress.

We saw substantial *growth* in product sales. We went from 100 to 2000 units sold in a month.

Climb – To reach new heights, literally or figuratively

Our sales *climbed* substantially the week before Christmas.

Improve – To actively make something better than its current state.

We can *improve* our customer satisfaction scores across the board.

An Improvement - A positive change in a person, thing, or situation.

There was a huge *improvement* in our customer satisfaction scores.

Peak – The highest point of something. This can be a moment when something is in demand, at its highest value, or the tallest physical point of a structure.

Charles's opportunity to give a TED talk was the *peak* of his career.

The following words are used in a negative context or to present a problem:

Decline - A drop or fall in something, usually in reference to sales or specific behavior.

Our subscription rates saw a massive *decline* when our competitor had a Christmas promotion.

Decrease - When something shows less activity or less of an object.

We had a *decrease* in our online engagement last month and we're investigating to find out what happened.

A Drop - A sudden, downward change in numbers.

We saw a huge *drop* in sales last month so we need to recover this month.

Reduce - To make something smaller or less expensive.

I advise you to *reduce* the costs of production by five percent so your products can drop down in price.

A great way to describe something is with adverbs. These words tell us how something happened and usually end in -ly. They're great to practice before a presentation.

Dramatically – By a large amount.

The company's community outreach *greatly* improved morale and our public image.

Sharply – By a steep angle that changed by a sudden amount.

Sales went up *sharply* when we focused on our female customers.

Enormously – By a surprising amount, more than expected.

Our workflow changed *enormously* with this new program.

Substantially – By a large amount, but not so much that it surprised anyone.

Our following on social media platforms went up *substantially,* but I think we can still do better.

Considerably – By a noticeable amount, but nothing impressive.

We have *considerably* more clients on our waiting list ever since we released that video.

Moderately – By a small amount.

Last year our sales went up *moderately*, but we believe we can quadruple those numbers this year.

Slightly – By a small, almost unnoticeable amount.

Unfortunately, that advertising campaign only raised sales *slightly,* from eight percent to 10 percent.

Steadily – In a regular manner without any big jumps or drops.

I'm happy to say that our online group is growing *steadily*; we get about ten new members every week.

Suddenly – In a quick, unexpected way.

Just as we got settled into the new office, *suddenly* we got hit with three massive orders.

Rapidly – At a very fast pace

We saw sales peak *rapidly*, so much that we couldn't meet the demand.

Significantly – In an important way and worthy of attention.

We watched our online engagement go up *significantly* after the article was released.

Exercise: A Practice Presentation

Directions: Read through the presentation below and replace the text in parentheses (_) with an adverb or one of your vocabulary words. For example: We were happy to see our order rate increase (in an important way) this quarter! Answer: (significantly)

Hello, good morning everyone. I want to talk to you about some of our findings from our online community that my colleagues and I believe could be indicators of some important (popular changes).

Let's take a look.

Here you can see the group reached its (highest point) in November. Members engaged with our content (by a regular amount) each day and gave us some great feedback. From their comments, we learned that mindfulness and wellness are a top concern for most, particularly at work.

Compared to the past five years, attitudes around mental health in the office changed (by a surprising amount). This (evidence of progress) seems to have come about (in a quick, unexpected way), but if we look at the shift in attitudes toward mental health, it isn't so surprising.

Overall, what we learned is that workers want to see their offices (actively make something better) and emphasize health and well-being. They want meditation rooms, healthy foods, even yoga breaks to help them keep their blood pumping.

Companies who refuse to offer these benefits are likely to see a (sudden, downward change), in applications.

That's all I have for you today. Thank you.

NEGOTIATION LANGUAGE

Every person has to negotiate as part of their every day life. A secretary might need to adjust their hours, a boss might have to ask employees to come in over the weekend, or a middle manager might want a raise. In order to ask for what we want, we have to be able to negotiate at work.

A negotiation is a request that implies you can do something for the person helping you in return for getting what you want. For example, if you want a higher salary, you may have to offer to help new employees with training or move into a leadership role. If you want to work from home one day a week, you may need to help the boss with a big presentation first.

To be a good negotiator is to be a good worker. Don't underestimate this essential skill. It can further your career in one conversation.

Consult – To seek information or advice from someone with experience in that field.

We need to *consult* finance to see if these changes are still within the overall budget.

Recap – To state again as a summary.

Let's *recap* the details from our meeting last week.

Reconvene – To meet again after taking a break.

Let's stop here for a break and *reconvene* at 3pm.

Interrupt Someone – To start to talk when someone else hasn't finished.

I try not to interrupt anyone while they are speaking.

Tactics – Strategies used to gain a desired result.

I know you've worked with us before. What *tactics* do you recommend we try to sign more contracts?

Interest – To make one or more people interested in what you're doing or saying.

This information might *interest* you.

Contingency – Something that could happen in the future, but there is no guarantee.

You might need to stay overnight in Houston, so you have an extra 500 dollars in your budget for *contingencies*.

Unanimous – To be in full agreement with two or more people.

The decision to work a four-day work week was *unanimous*.

Binding - Part of a legal agreement that cannot be broken by either side.

Business contracts are intended to be legally *binding*.

Tactful – A person who has the ability to do or say something without offending others.

The CEO was *tactful* while discussing the changes within the organization.

Mutual – A reciprocal agreement in the idea of an exchange or balance between two or more people or groups.

They always have *mutual* respect for one another.

Face-to-Face – A situation in which you see someone in person.

I'd prefer to meet *face-to-face* to discuss this with you.

Non-Negotiable – An item that is not open for further discussion or changes.

This decision is *non-negotiable*.

The following section covers conditional phrases in negotiations. These are polite, formal phrases you can use when asking for a different position or a higher salary at work. We use these phrases when we understand that in order to get what we want, we'll have to give something in return.

As Long As – An action that complements another action from a second person.

We are willing to meet you halfway *as long as* the price can be locked in for the next three years.

On the Condition That – A stipulation or requirement that is specified as part of an agreement.

We'd like to hire you *on the condition that* you sign a two-year contract with us.

Provided That – A rule you have to follow to get what you want.

You may go to the conference *provided that* you keep up with your work remotely while you're gone.

Supposing – If by way of hypothesis, on the assumption that.

Supposing I did that presentation for you, would that change your mind?

SMALL TALK AND NETWORKING

Networking – The action or process of interacting with others to exchange information and develop professional or social contacts. Networking often takes place in an informal setting and is vital in developing a successful career.

Whenever you attend a conference, meet a visitor in the office, or get to know a new person, it can be helpful to learn a bit of small talk.

Small talk, or basic, polite conversation can help two or more people have a chat without discussing anything important. It tends to be about unimportant things like what someone is drinking, the weather outside, or someone's agenda for the day.

Here are some commonly used questions and expressions to help you navigate small talk in and out of the office:

Greetings:

Hi, I'm _____. What's your name?

What brought you here today?

What a nice venue. Have you been here before?

How's your day going?

Polite questions:

How'd you hear about this event?

How long have you been a member of this organization?

I was really impressed by the speech you made.

Are you from around here or did you travel to the event?

Care to join me?

What do you do?

When it's time to say goodbye

It's so nice to run into you.

It was great meeting you. Enjoy the conference.

Have a great time!

SOCIAL MEDIA TERMS

It's important to know how to speak about social media because more and more companies rely on their social media profiles and online communities to keep people interested. No matter what industry you plan to go into, you will need to at least discuss what's happening on the company's social media in order to help out at work.

Of course, these phrases can also be a huge help outside of work.

Viral – Videos, pictures or pieces of information that circulate rapidly and widely from one internet user to another. Many popular videos go viral and attract a lot of attention where people are talking about them.

I can't believe our company's video went *viral*! That's so exciting!

Social Media Platform – Social media platforms allow users to create an account and share user-generated contact that includes information, videos and pictures.

TikTok and Facebook are both *social media platforms*, even though they look very different.

Authentic – Real, genuine.

The key to a great Instagram is to be *authentic* and be who you truly are.

Influence – To cause someone to change a belief, behavior or opinion.

Creating an online community for open discussion about our company could greatly *influence* how we move forward.

Hashtag – A word or phrase preceded by a hash sign (#), used on social media websites and applications.

Our new *hashtag*, #moneymoves, rolls out on Monday.

Trending – Currently popular or widely discussed online, especially on social media websites.

Have you seen the boss's article on LinkedIn is *trending*?

Blog – A regularly updated website or web page, typically one run by an individual or small group, that is written in an informal or conversational style.

Our company's *blog* needs to be updated, I propose we hire a writer to keep it current.

User-Generated Content – Any form of content, such as images, videos, text, and audio, posted by users on online platforms such as social media.

Ever since we started posting Instagram challenges on our company account, we have a ton of *user-generated content!*

Post – A piece of writing, image, or other item of content published online, typically on a blog or social media website.

We need to brainstorm some future *posts* with our social media manager.

Social Media Manager - A new position at most companies. This person handles the company's online presence and helps them stay relevant with images, videos and blog posts.

Our new *social media manager* has an idea for some new content we can use to our advantage.

Exercise: Answer the following questions as best you can either with a language partner or by writing them in a notebook.

Have you or anyone you know ever gone viral? If yes, describe the video, (don't say the title), in a voice note to a friend and see if he/she can find it online. If not, do you think it would be fun or terrible to go viral? Explain your answer.

Imagine you have to write a blog for your company. Brainstorm five ideas for content in a mind map.

What do you think a person can do to be authentic online? Does it bother you if someone seems too perfect on the internet? Why or why not?

ENTREPRENEURSHIP VOCABULARY

How can we talk about people in the business world who work to change the world we live in? By learning entrepreneurship vocabulary! If you want to be able to chat with others in your field, start a business of your own, or discuss changes in your business, this is a great list of terms to practice.

Entrepreneurship – The activity of setting up a business or businesses, taking on financial risks in the hope of profit. Entrepreneurship allows individuals to create their own career path by developing products or services that people need and want.

It requires a certain level of *entrepreneurship* to pursue the dream of starting your own business, but I believe you can do it.

Entrepreneur – A person who organizes and operates a business and takes on greater than normal financial risks to do so and often receives a larger salary. Many people dream of being an entrepreneur, however starting your own business is difficult and only those who persevere will succeed.

I met the owner of my favorite doughnut chain yesterday. I had no idea he was such an *entrepreneur*!

Business Incubators – An organization designed to help startup companies and individual entrepreneurs to develop their businesses by offering a full range of services and support resources that could include physical space, capital, coaching, common services, and networking connections.

In order to get into our *business incubator*, you need to pitch us an idea for a new app or small business and have it approved.

Startup Accelerators/Seed Accelerators – Fixed-term, cohort-based programs that include mentorship and educational components and culminate in a public pitch event or demo day.

I had a chance to join an incubator, but I think I prefer a *seed accelerator*.

Angel Investor – Individuals who offer promising startup companies funding in exchange for a piece of the business, usually in the form of equity or royalties.

Our *angel investors* now have access to our financial reports from the past six months and moving forward.

Venture Capitalists – a person who makes capital investments in companies in exchange for an equity stake. The venture capitalist is often expected to bring managerial and technical expertise, as well as capital, to their investments.

We need a *venture capitalist* who understands our vision for a new kind of video call.

Crowdfunding – The use of small amounts of capital from a large number of people. The traditional circle includes owners, relatives and venture capitalists.

If you can't get a venture capitalist to put capital behind your idea, try *crowdfunding*. Sometimes consumers understand new ideas better than others.

Bootstrapping – Building a company from the ground up with nothing but personal savings, and with luck, the cash coming in from the first sales. The term is also used as a noun: A bootstrap is a business an entrepreneur launches with little or no outside cash or other support.

Remy's new bakery will require a lot of *bootstrapping* from him, but he says he's up for it.

Operating Revenues – The revenue that a company generates from its primary business activities. For example, a retailer produces its operating revenue through merchandise sales. Furthermore, a physician derives their operating revenue from the medical services that they provide.

Our *operating revenues* were almost nothing last year, but this quarter looks more profitable.

Innovative – New and original products, services and ideas. Technology has many innovative products as advancements happen quickly.

This new app is a more *innovative* approach to video-making as it adjusts the lights in-camera, making everyone look better.

In Demand – Sought after. When products or services are in demand then many people want them. It's great for an entrepreneur to have products that are in high demand.

Congratulations on being acquired, your products are so *in demand*!

Plan of Action – An organized program of measures to be taken in order to achieve a goal. Entrepreneurs need to have a *plan of action* to succeed. Having a business plan that can be measured will help guide the process.

Before I can leave my job to start my own company, I need a solid *plan of action*.

Business Venture – A new business that is formed with a plan and expectation that financial gain will follow. It can be referred to as a small business and usually has few financial resources. Small *business ventures* are similar to startups, but the main difference is the expectation of growth; startups are meant to grow fast.

My new *business venture* attracted so many investors.

Opportunity – An avenue of activity that is both actionable and has the potential to provide value to an entrepreneur and to customers.

I got a great *opportunity* to run the blog of a major corporation.

Acquisition – When one company purchases most or all of another company's shares to gain control of that company.

We're planning an *acquisition* of our biggest competitor to take advantage of their algorithms.

Strategy – A plan of action or policy designed to achieve a major or overall aim.

What's your *strategy* to make your company more profitable in the next five years?

Valuation – An estimation of something's worth, especially one carried out by a professional appraiser.

The *valuation* of Tom's company was over four million.

Equity – The value of the shares issued by a company. Shown on a balance sheet and will show a company's financial health.

I'll invest in your startup, but I want 30 percent *equity*.

Revenue – The money generated from normal business operations, calculated as the average sales price times the number of units sold.

Our *revenue* this year was high enough to give the staff bonuses for the holiday.

Untapped Market – When there's a demand for a product or service that isn't being supplied by any company yet. This provides businesses an opportunity to be the first brand offering a product or service.

We believe our school lunch planning app lets us inside an *untapped market*.

Traction – The progress of a start-up company and the momentum it gains as the business grows.

You should contact some venture capitalists now while you have some good *traction*.

Distribution Channel – A chain of businesses or intermediaries through which a good or service passes until it reaches the final buyer or the end consumer. *Distribution channels* can include wholesalers, retailers, distributors and even the internet.

Show me your toy company's *distribution channel*.

Investment – The action or process of investing money for profit or material result.

I'd like to make a fifty thousand dollar *investment* in the capital markets.

Innovators – A person who introduces new methods, ideas or products.

As an angel investor, it makes me really excited to meet a true *innovator* who can reimagine the way we do things.

Early Adopters – A person who starts using a product or technology as soon as it becomes available.

My husband stands in line for hours to get a new gadget. He prides himself on being an *early adopter*.

Elevator Pitch – A brief way to introduce yourself to someone using key information while making a connection with someone.

I need to practice my *elevator pitch* before I go to the big tech conference in Brazil.

Industry Analysis – Looking at how your company compares to others that are in the same niche.

I did an *industry analysis*. It looks like the existing companies have a blind spot when it comes to marketing - they all rely on referrals.

Market Analysis – Studying the attractiveness and the dynamics of a special market within a specific industry.

According to our *market analysis*, parents spend over one hundred thousand dollars per kid on snacks alone.

Customer Acquisition – A set of techniques used to manage customer prospects and inquiries generated by marketing. Customer acquisition management can be considered the connection between advertising and customer relationship management to acquire new customers.

Mary did a great job increasing our *customer acquisition*. Her new campaign doubled our client list!

Marketing Strategy – A plan of action designed to promote and sell a product or service. Businesses use a number of *marketing strategies* to help them grow.

We have a new *marketing strategy* that uses old-school techniques like stickers and fliers with the website's name.

Business Model – A design for the successful operation of a business, identifying revenue sources, customer base, products and details of financing.

We love the Google *business model* of putting employees' needs first.

Financial Projections – A model that projects either the current year or a rolling 12-month period.

This financial projection shows that we stand to make a 12 percent increase this year.

Monetization Plan – A plan to generate revenue for your product.

I've made these dolls for free for years, but my daughter wants me to try her *monetization plan* and turn them into a small business.

Sole Proprietorship – An unincorporated business that has just one owner who pays personal income tax on profits earned from the business.

Right now I'm the only one in my business, so I'm registering it as a *sole proprietorship*.

Partnership – A formal arrangement by two or more parties to manage and operate a business and share its profits.

I think it would benefit our company and theirs if we created a *partnership*.

Corporation - A company or group of people authorized to act as a single entity and recognized as such in law.

I understand the boss wants to take our satellite locations and recategorize them all as one corporation.

Exercise: True or false. Read each statement and decide if each one is correct, (T for true), incorrect, (F for false).

1. Example: A corporation is a small business run by a few individuals. <u>F</u>

2. An industry analysis can show you more about how your competitors make money. _____

3. Crowdfunding helps you get money when you need it for something expensive you want to buy. _____

4. A problem in your distribution channel won't affect your business. Just ignore it. _____

5. The dream of every entrepreneur is to find an untapped market, one where no one else is working to make money. _____

6. A business model is a beautiful woman who sells office furniture. _____

MOTIVATING EMPLOYEES

If you need to talk about management, office morale, or anything related to motivation for employees, these are the phrases you need to learn.

Intrinsic Motivation – A behavior that produces an internal reward. The behavior is driven by the person because the internal benefit it will produce is satisfying. An example would be someone who exercises for a burst of dopamine.

Some people have tons of *intrinsic motivation* and have had amazing achievements..

Extrinsic Motivation – Motivation that stems directly from rewards. It is reward-driven behavior. These rewards can be financial, such as pay raises, bonuses, or commission. There are also non-financial rewards that include promotions, recognition, praise, or an important project assignment.

Our city wants to give an award to the most ecologically-minded company this year and I think we can win it. That would be great *extrinsic motivation!*

Progress – Forward or onward movement toward a destination.

David, you made a lot of *progress* with your training this past month.

Confidence – A feeling of self-assurance arising from one's appreciation of one's own abilities or qualities. A belief someone has in their own abilities.

My *confidence* has grown as I continue to have more experience with presenting.

Micromanage – A boss or manager who gives excessive supervision to employees and may feel the need to watch over their shoulder and contribute to every decision.

I am going to let my team make the necessary decisions they need to and I won't *micromanage* them.

Lead by Example – To act in a way that shows others how to behave. The best leaders choose to lead by example.

When I worked in a cafe one summer, our manager would *lead by example*. He even mopped the floors himself.

Accessible – Available and easy to speak to or deal with in a friendly manner.

Pam is so *accessible*. She's available when I need some advice.

Push Limits – Trying to do a little more than what's allowed, without suffering consequences.

The boss really wants to *push the limits* of our sales team.

Find Out – To discover new information or learn more about a person or topic.

I need you to *find out* more about our upcoming event, I would like to be a part of it.

Extra Credit:

There are tons of things a boss can do to motivate employees, but more than anything, people want to be seen and heard at work. No one likes to be a faceless drone in a crowd. A boss who respects their team and gives them the time to say how they feel or what they think will always get better work from everyone.

Here's a quick list of some basic things a leader can do to keep everyone on track.

As a boss it's important to:

Pay employees what they're worth

Encourage personal growth through trainings in and out of the company

Get to know the team members as individuals

Encourage your team to innovate and find new solutions to persistent problems

Follow through with any promises or rewards

Help your team make a difference in the community with a volunteer activity like building homes or working a day at a soup kitchen.

Avoid the temptation to schedule non-stop meetings. If work is quiet it's because things are going well.

Admit any mistakes on your part. Your team will thank you by being more honest with you as well.

CONCLUSION

You've learned a lot of great vocabulary and phrases to get you speaking more naturally at work. As a language teacher, I know how much effort it requires to learn everything from this book and practicing in a professional setting will help. You will do well and achieve everything you have set out to do.

So, I want to give you some advice moving forward.

Let your colleagues know you're learning idioms or specific business associated terms

Most native speakers know someone who has English as a second language. It's not uncommon for Americans, Canadians, or Australians to have someone in their life that tends to make tiny mistakes with their language. The best thing you can do as a learner is to take advantage of this situation and let them know you're learning new terms. It also makes for interesting conversation because native speakers often assume that everyone knows or has learned these terms from this book.

If someone at work comes up to you and starts chatting away and uses an expression you've never heard before, ask them questions or clarify the meaning by using, "So what you're saying is ………." Try saying something similar to this to make sure you understand the meaning.

As long as you're polite and patient, most people will be patient and polite with you.

Find a language partner or hire a teacher for private lessons

Language partners can be either a person learning English as well or someone who wants to practice your native language with you in exchange for some English practice. For example, if your first language is Spanish, you can do an exchange with a coworker who wants to practice her Spanish for some help with English. The two of you could practice Spanish for thirty minutes in the morning, then do another half hour of English in the afternoon.

Language partners are a great resource for keeping you motivated and helping you hear yourself speak out loud. You're much more likely to keep up with your English studies with a little pressure from a friend or a colleague. A language partner can also check your pronunciation and help you hear where to emphasize a word or part of a word. Plus, it makes learning much more fun.

Set realistic goals for yourself

Language goals are a bit different from personal or professional goals as they are specific tasks you want to accomplish in English. While a personal goal might be, "I want to vacation in Puerto Vallarta next summer," a language goal can be, "I want to order food, without help, at that fancy restaurant my friends like."

Set two or three goals for yourself each month and ask your language partner to help you stay focused on your achievements. Here are a few goals to get you started:

- I want to tell a joke in English and get a big laugh
- I will order a fancy coffee at my favorite cafe
- I want to make a phone call to a friend and have a conversation for at least five minutes
- I plan to watch a movie in English without subtitles
- I will go on a date with someone who only speaks English

Keep track of your progress and any unexpected issues. If you find your joke unexpectedly offends someone or if your coffee order comes back to you all wrong, talk to someone about it and figure out what you can do differently next time.

Remember, mistakes are embarrassing for a moment, but they help you memorize your vocabulary words for a lifetime!

Make flashcards

Flashcards are a great resource for studying on your own or with a friend. All you need is a set of notecards and an afternoon to make them.

Use a nice marketer to write a vocabulary word, phrase, or idiom on one side, then the definition on the other. Once you're done, you have a powerful memorization tool that can boost your English skills significantly.

Here are some quick flashcard activities:

Stack your cards up in one big pile, then put down scraps of paper marked 1, 2, 3, and 4 in a row across your space, with number one above your starting stack of cards. Pick up the first card, read the word, and try to define it. If you get it right, move it to space two. If you get it wrong, put it on the bottom of the stack under number 1. Continue with the next card. Every time you get a definition right, the card moves down the line. As soon as you get it wrong, it stays in one place. The cards that end up at number four are the words you know well, so take them out and start again with the remaining cards. Do this until every flashcard moves down to the last spot.

Have a language partner take your cards and hold them up one by one, the vocabulary word facing you and the definition facing your partner. You have to read the word, then use it in a sentence. Your partner checks to make sure your sentence is correct with the help of the definition. Every word you get right is a point for you, wrong is a point for your partner. Whomever has the most points at the end of the run is the winner.

Use your cards as clues for pictionary. Get two teams together, at least two to five people per team, then set up a whiteboard or big drawing pad and markers or pens. Divide your vocabulary flashcards in half and give one half to the other team.

Here's how you play - the first artist takes a card from the top of the pile and doesn't let his/her team see the word. Then, the other team starts a timer for two minutes. The artist needs to draw clues on his/her board to help their teammates guess the word before the timer goes off. Teammates can yell out their guesses, but the artist cannot speak while he/she draws. If the teammates guess the correct word, they get a point, but if they guess incorrectly, they get no points. Then, the other team gets a turn.

MORE RESOURCES FOR ENGLISH

It's important to find lots of different ways to practice your new language. Here are a few great places on the web, books, and other ideas to keep you sharp.

Websites

- Cambridge Online Dictionary - One of the best resources online. Get definitions, phonetic pronunciations, translations, and any disparities between American and British English.

- News in Levels - A site that turns news stories into mini English lessons. Choose from levels 1, 2, or 3 to practice your language and keep up with current events.

- FluentU - A wonderful site that helps visitors find one another, gives you fun articles to read and a free newsletter to join for better practice.

- Five Minute English - Handy, quick lessons for students for fast study sessions.

- AmigosIngleses.com - A great site for native Spanish speakers with fun videos to watch, resources to help you practice your listening, and more.

Books

- English Collocations in Use - To master English and sound as natural as possible, you need to know your collocations. These tricky phrases get a thorough breakdown in this easy-to-read textbook for intermediate-level learners.

- English Grammar in Use, (the version with answers) - One of the top grammar books available in the world, this book gives simple, clear explanations for confusing grammar points. The exercises are a huge help. This volume comes in three levels; beginner, intermediate, and advanced.

- Practical English Usage - A grammar book designed for English language learners. This resource keeps the explanations short and simple.

If you don't want another textbook and just need a good story, there are some wonderful fiction books for language learners that teachers love to recommend.

Check out my favorite titles:

- The Compound Effect - a book about how small changes over a long period of time make a big impact.

- The Magic of Thinking Big - a book about how our thinking will affect the trajectory of our lives.

- The Alchemist - A story about following your dream to find your purpose in life.

- The Ultimate Jim Rohn Library- An audiobook dedicated to mining the skills and talents you have.

Other great resources

If you want to do something a little different, you can always find more social ways to practice your language skills.

Try one of these options to help you improve your conversation skills:

- Chat with someone on an app - this pressures you to answer questions and ask some of your own. We use more slang and colloquial phrases in chats, so they can be a good way to practice more casual English.

- Join a conversation club - Try finding a group devoted to language practice that is not a class. These groups tend to be more relaxed and fun as they don't involve evaluations. Most conversation clubs meet in public places and accept people of all levels. Most of them focus on games to get everyone speaking.

- Talk to yourself - There's no pressure to get it exactly right and you're always available to yourself. You can look in the mirror or speak into your phone and record yourself if you want to listen to your progress. However you do it, use this practice as a chance to carry on a complex conversation without the stress.

Whatever you choose as your means to practice English, we hope you find a way to use your new language everyday. Remember, language grows with you and the more you use it the more it can do for you. Your hard work will pay off in more opportunities, great friendships, and a chance to lead the way for other language learners.

Milton Keynes UK
Ingram Content Group UK Ltd.
UKHW031618231124
451036UK00004B/52